Praise for *Art Is A___ ___g Whole*

"A heartfelt and nourishing book about the way that art can surround and support your life. If you feel like you're outside the art world, if the art world isn't helping you, this book can be a life ring ... Put it around you, and you'll be towed safely into shore."

— James Elkins, author of *Pictures and Tears: A History of People Who Have Cried in Front of Paintings*

"In *Art Is About Being Whole: A Memoir*, Cindy Ingram takes us on a remarkable journey through the world of art and her own personal transformation. Her story of healing and self-discovery is a testament to the power of art to mend, enlighten, and empower. I felt this book in my heart. I always knew that art could heal in a deep way, but through this book, that became manifest. The way I look at and appreciate art has been forever changed as a result."

— Elizabeth Kilpatrick, Sr. Vice President, Geena Davis Institute on Gender in Media

"*Art Is About Being Whole* is a profound testament to the transformative power of art in one's life, ... and an invitation to explore the vast landscapes of your own emotions through the lens of art. In its pages, you'll discover that there is no one truth with art, but rather a multitude of truths waiting for you to embrace. This book is a beautifully crafted reminder of the art's potential to bring healing, clarity, and, most importantly, a profound sense of wholeness to our lives."

— Jacob Nordby, author of *The Creative Cure: How Finding and Freeing Your Inner Artist Can Heal Your Life*

"*Art Is About Being Whole* is a song of praise, celebration, and invitation—into the power of art to illuminate and expand our lived lives. Cindy Ingram's memoir shares her story as a testament to the ways a full embrace of art can heal our injured places, illuminate our uncertainties, and open doors of experience that we never imagined. A beautiful book filled with ideas to be inspired by and to borrow. You will feel you have new best friends in Cindy and a thousand artists when you finish."

— Eric Booth, Founder of International Teaching Artist Collaborative and author of *Making Change* and *Tending the Perennials*

"With compassion, understanding, and beauty, Cindy Ingram has written a mesmerizing guide for finding yourself no matter how lost or broken you might be feeling. If you've ever felt like you didn't belong or are safe in your own skin, Cindy masterfully walks you through how to rediscover yourself through art and reflection."

— Dayna Abraham, author of *Calm the Chaos: A Failproof Roadmap for Parenting Even the Most Challenging Kids*

"If you are lucky, once in a blue moon, a portal opens up, and it rearranges and upgrades how you see and make sense of the world inside and around you in ways that awaken you to a special kind of magic. *Art Is About Being Whole*, the debut memoir by Cindy Ingram, is that portal, and entering it will activate in you the kind of curiosity, imagination, clarity, and inspiration that you did not know you needed. Through the most potent blend of bravery, vulnerability, humor, and poetry, intuitively and gracefully weaved together inside a bold, rich, and cozy artistic frame, Cindy takes us along on a journey of self-discovery where she finds healing, love, and a deep remembrance of her unique magic in the most unlikely of places and ways."
— Yola Mehmeti, Energy Healer, Writer, Teacher

"*Art Is About Being Whole: A Memoir* is a beautiful and raw account of the power of art to heal, give clarity, hold space, and do magic. Cindy Ingram has truly outdone herself with this book. She invites the reader into her lived experience with humor, humility, and wisdom. Along the way, she seamlessly weaves contemporary and historical artworks into her personal stories, creating a true literary masterpiece. Let this book be the delightful punch in your gut that reminds you to listen to your heart. Settle in and get comfortable. It's impossible to put down."
— Dr. Sarah Ackermann, Executive Director for Teaching Innovation at Ball State University and Supervision and Administration Division Director-Elect for the National Art Education Association

"In her visually delicious memoir, Cindy Ingram reminds us that we all have the capacity to open our hearts, to be touched and held by art in a way that helps us meet, love, and heal ourselves. A beauty-full and relatable memoir for any person craving to connect to the wholeness of true self. And OMG the visuals, art, and poetry will enliven your soul—you might even swoon. I know I did."
— Allison Crow, Coach and author of *Unarmored: Finding Home in the Wild Edges of Being Human*

"*Art Is About Being Whole* captivates the reader with its raw vulnerability and poetic words, soothing, disrupting, energizing, and helping us to re-awaken those parts of ourselves that are transformed by encounters with works of art. Ingram exposes the power of art-encounters that occur within the lived experience. She invites us to attend to her more personal moments with specific works of art, as she traces the influence of these pivot points in her thinking, doing, and own art-making ... holding the reader in a space of magic and enchantment, but also in empathy and compassion. This is a story of healing and finding the self; it is a story of those in-between, not-quite-tangible experiences with art that move the spirit to dig deeper, to look harder, to let go, and to accept what shows up in life as one moves through it."
— Kate Wurtzel, Ph.D., Artist, Researcher, and Assistant Professor of Art Education

"From the moment I read the words '... in front of art I knew I belonged. I felt held. I felt welcomed,' I knew Ingram's work would be a transformational piece of literature that dug deep into my soul, revealed more of the beauty of who I am, and helped me to find the strength to share even more of myself through my art. Take this journey to wholeness as you read the beautifully woven story of a life fired, formed, molded by the power of art. I am confident this will be something I read over and over."

— Jed Dearybury, Educator, Author, Illustrator

"In *Art Is About Being Whole*, Cindy Ingram deftly employs art as an oracle and poetry as a self-help tool, leveraging these mediums to navigate her path toward healing and self-discovery. In the pages of this memoir, her generosity shines through as she offers this book as a way finder, a guiding compass for others embarking on their journey of self-exploration and transformation. So, they, too, can celebrate and claim themselves unbroken and whole."

— Glenis Redmond, author of *The Listening Skin*

"I have admired Cindy Ingram for some time, her ability to pivot from historian, to teacher, to entrepreneur, to life coach and now author. What I've admired more is her transparency and vulnerability about life all while weaving art into all aspects of it. This book is no different, there are teachings about art, life, and self that the reader will take to heart. [Her] writing cut straight through the mundane and right to my heart... Thank you, Cindy, for sharing your story with all of the unique strange people of the world."

— Laura Grundler, Arts Administrator and
Co-Founder of *K12ArtChat the Podcast*

"*Art Is About Being Whole: A Memoir* is an absolute must-read. Cindy Ingram shares her story in a raw and relatable manner. Her writing is authentic and captivating, intricately intersecting each story with art and philosophy. As a reader, I also loved the use of powerful questions to help me reflect and make connections in my personal life. This book will be an invaluable personal source, but one I will highly recommend to my clients as well."

— Dr. Charryse Johnson, LCMHC, Expert Mental Health Consultant
and author of *Expired Mindsets: Releasing Patterns That No Longer Serve You Well*

"Art making and art teaching at its best derive from deep personal explorations, creative experiences, and observations. *Art Is About Being Whole* defines meaningful connections between artmaking and being a whole human being: a caring, well-rounded, and creative soul. This is a book to be valued and cherished."

— Dr. George Szekely, Author, Professor Emeritus, and
Area Head of Art Education at University of Kentucky, Lexington

"What an incredible way to process emotions through works of art! This memoir conveys the beauty of being human in a messy world. Leading by beautiful example, Ingram displays how art has created space and healing throughout her life. A beautiful story for us all to admire."

— Kerry Hope, author of *Your Triple Goddess: A Path to Self-Love, Empowerment, and Healing*

"A stunningly intimate and original memoir about stepping into authority and authenticity in our own lives. Ingram's focus is art, and her passion for it is obvious. And how could it not be? Art has been the catalyst for her becoming whole, inside and out. I loved traveling with Ingram as she shared her journey through her most intimate (and sometimes painful) times of life, showing how art was an external mirror for her interior world. Read this book slowly. Wash yourself in the colors. Cover yourself with the poetry. See yourself in the pages. And let this book — really, a beautiful piece of art all by itself - heal you from the inside out."

— Angie Stegall, Wayfinder, Executive Coach, and Certified Forest Therapy Guide

"...a beautiful dive into how art can open up healing and perspectives to enrich our lives in ways many may not have ever considered. Ingram beautifully shares her healing journey with depth and honesty, captivating the reader with every word on the page. Her insights into how art provided a gateway back to who she was and how it allowed her to touch the deepest parts of herself took my breath away. Ingram's story welcomes readers to explore their own tucked-away emotions and the gifts that can be found when we allow ourselves to deeply feel and connect to the parts of us that need love and attention."

— Lisa Carpenter, Coach, Author, Speaker, and WBFF Professional Athlete

"As an author of books offering process art for children, I found Ingram's book not only inspiring but affirming. Freedom to create without boundaries matters for the human spirit, young and old! Open creativity reaches deep into the heart and soul as Ingram details through her artistic journey."

— MaryAnn F. Kohl, Author and Educator, brightring.com

❋ ❋ ❋

ART IS ABOUT BEING WHOLE

A Memoir

Cindy Ingram

**Compassionate Mind
Collaborative**

cmcollab.com

Published by Compassionate Mind Collaborative

**Compassionate Mind
Collaborative**
cmcollab.com

Edited by Heather Doyle Fraser
Cover and interior design and layout by Rachel Lapp Whitt
Cover art by Cindy Ingram
Proofed by Christie Robb
Marketing by Jesse Sussman
Author Photo by Me Ra Koh, Cofounder of Fioria

ISBN: 979-8-9869419-1-2 (paperback)
ISBN: 979-8-9869419-2-9 (ebook)

This paperback edition first published in 2023.

For the artists
whose bravery, vulnerability, and creative spirit
have reached across the void and given me a
place of refuge when I needed it most.

and

To Eric, Lily, and Zoey
For being my catalyst and my safe space
as I found my wings

Contents

Introduction:
Circle of Life

Art, like love, just is.
Giving, Receiving, Asking
for nothing. Just whole.

It's a scene we all know. The sun rises over the African savannah into a brightening red-orange sky—waves of heat distorting the star as it ascends above the horizon. This sun, which rises and sets each day but doesn't ever cease to captivate with its majesty. The iconic scene continues by showing the expansiveness of our world—the immense open sky, the massive waterfalls, the fog hovering on the ground with a snow-capped mountain behind. Rays of sunlight cut through the scene and reflect off of a lake. The large and small animals unite together and bow to their new king. As we watch, our emotions surge at the beautiful song written and composed by Tim Rice and Elton John (1994) and soulfully sung by Carmen Twillie with the Zulu vocals of Lebo M. repeating in the background—"*ingonyama nengw'enamabala.*" The song's lyrics remind me of the magnificence of life—

"more to see than can ever be seen,
more to do than can ever be done...
more to find than can ever be found"
and all of the emotions available for us to feel—
"through despair and hope,
through faith and love."

"Circle of Life" from Disney®'s *The Lion King* has always mesmerized me, and when the movie came out in eighth grade, I saw it twelve times at the theater. I lived around the corner from the dollar movie theater, and my now lifelong friend Jeanne and I would walk over and watch it again and again. And I would cry every time at the opening—moved by the swell of the music, the grandness of the setting, the emotion of the vocals, the connectedness of the animals, and the poetry and relevance of the lyrics. I didn't know then that I was having my first truly connected sublime experience with art. From that point on, I chased that feeling, chasing it again and again by showing up at the theater with my dollar plus tax and pockets filled with snacks, and then chased it as I grew up seeking out art experiences where I would feel held by the art, safe as I explored the feelings of awe, wonder, and connectedness.

✳ ✳ ✳

It was a movie scene in eighth grade that first allowed me to go here, but as I grew older, I found most of these moving experiences would happen with works of art hanging in museums and galleries around the world. The art would stop me and hold my attention as firmly as "Circle of Life." In that pristine moment, an expansive swell fills my chest. Tears spring to my eyes. The art transfixes me, and I cannot look away. Sometimes my legs feel weak or wobbly. My heart rate and breathing speed up to keep up with the emotion taking over my body. It's not an out-of-body experience but a full-body one.

Every part of me is with the art. And then I stay there for as long as I can. Captivated. My mind wanders as my eyes travel around the art—trying to memorize every piece of the artwork, curious about what created the feeling, curious about what message the artwork has for me, and open to receiving all I can from this powerful experience. I think about myself and where I am in life, how my life relates to the artwork, and I also wonder about the artist—how did they think and feel as they created it? What was the process like for them? I marvel at the human need to communicate who and what we are through visual imagery. How the visual can capture things that words cannot. I think about the others who have also stood before this same artwork minutes or years before and its impact on them.

These moments are pure connection—to myself, to the art, to the artist, to everyone else who has ever seen the art, to humanity at large, to the soul and spirit of the earth and everyone on it. It's the closest I have ever gotten to a spiritual experience, but there is no bright light or opening heavens. There is no harp music or people breaking into song. As I look around, the environment is the same as before. Even though I feel frozen in time, people are moving around and unaware of the explosion happening inside my brain and body. This experience is deeply personal: I feel it in my body, I feel it in my soul, and I feel it in every part of me. It overtakes me. It is both peaceful and tumultuous. It is bliss. My whole world picks itself up, shifts a little, and puts itself back down rearranged. All of the same parts are present, but somehow things are different now.

The art has changed me.

* * *

For most of my life, I have never felt safe—showing who I am, expressing feelings, feeling loved, and feeling liked even. If people knew who I really was, they would leave me. If I inconvenienced them with my feelings or was "too much" for them, they would be annoyed and not want me around. I felt like an alien in a human world, not understanding why I didn't fit in or why I felt so different. So I stuffed it all in—buried the spectrum of unsafe emotions and added layers onto my identity to hide the alien and become a more acceptable person—strike that—not just acceptable but exceptional and beyond reproach. But when I was in front of art, I knew I belonged. I felt held. I felt welcomed. My body would instantly relax when I entered a museum. There was no hiding. These big, silent, sacred spaces that are so intimidating or pretentious to many people give me the space and the expansiveness to feel whatever comes up without fear.

My body slows, my mind slows, and I can just be with—with art and with myself.

A Memoir Built with Art

This book explores the journey of finding who I am underneath all those layers of protection—what parts of me are real and what parts of me are there to make myself feel more worthy of love and acceptance. How do I do this? Through the art of course. That's how I relate to most meaningful things after all. Each vignette or essay incorporates a work of art that encapsulates the growth I have experienced at pivotal moments in my life. Each piece of art is a touch point for me to come back to again and again as I acknowledge where I've been and where I'm headed. From a Great White Shark swimming stealthily beneath my burnout to a futuristic painting of a mask connecting me with the humanity of my long-lost biological father to a succession of painted eyes clarifying my spirituality, each artwork in this book helps me put words and images to thoughts, feelings, and transformations that often feel too hard to explain with words.

How do you explain a feeling? That's what artists do.

My Hope for You

I write this book to illustrate how art is more than just something to appreciate or learn about or look at, but that it has the power to heal, give clarity, hold space, and do magic. In my darkest times, deep in grief, anxiety, depression, and shame, art has always been there for me. It was how I experienced the fullness of life and the depths of connection before I did all of this work to come to a place of wholeness. A place where I feel like I know and love who I am, without shame, without feeling the need to pretend to be something else, without the constant need to fix my broken self. Using works of art to show this is a natural choice because I have dedicated my entire life to sharing the magic of art with anyone who will listen, and now, that is you.

I hope as you read these pages and be with these artworks, you find a safe place for you—safe with the art that I explore in the book and safe with me as I share my heart with you.

When I look at an artwork, I am compelled to put myself into it, to find my place in it. My interpretations of these artworks in this book are 100 percent my own. I am not presuming to know the pain or internal world of the artist. I am not saying that my interpretation is the truth—your interpretation is just as true, as is the artist's. When the artwork (or the book) leaves the artist's hands, it becomes the viewer's (or the reader's). It is a gift from the artist to the viewer.

There is no one truth with art. The only truth is the one you find inside of you. I have become a more true version of myself during this writing process. Now, I invite you to use my story and these artworks as tools to find the truest version of you.

An Invitation for You, Reader

Art is a gift, but it is also an invitation for deeper connection. If this work resonates with you, I invite you to download the art connection guide to accompany the artworks in this book at https://artandself.com/book. The guide will lead you through your own discovery and connection to the works. Also available at that same link is a book club guide with a twist—use this book with your book club, and instead of a traditional discussion of the book, I will show you how to weave art discussions into your gathering. And of course, I invite you to listen to the *Art and Self Podcast* to hear my deep and authentic conversations about art with various insightful and delightful people https://artandself.com/podcast.

And for the most profound connection to yourself and to art, I'd love to have you in my program, the *Art Connection Circle* (https://artandself.com/circle). The *Art Connection Circle* is an intimate group program where we look at meaningful art and participate in a variety of introspective activities in community. The group program weaves together art appreciation, self-development, and compassionate creativity to create a powerful program of self-discovery, intimate community, and deep connection to the human spirit. The core purpose of the program is to help you find the most true version of yourself through art, just as I do in this book.

I have often wondered, does Art contain
all the answers I have been searching for?
I think I hear a whisper admist the chaos,
"What does wholeness look like?

Swoon (American, born 1977). *Thalassa*, 2011. Block print on paper with hand painted colors in acrylic gouache, mounted to wooden panels. Overall: 720 x 720 x 600 inches (1828.8 x 1828.8 x 1524 cm). Collection Buffalo AKG Art Museum. Gift of the artist (2020:13). © 2023 Swoon / Artists Rights Society (ARS), New York. Photo: Brenda Bieger, Buffalo AKG Art Museum

PART ONE

Within the Mess

Wholeness looks like being
free.
Embodied in the knowing
that who you are is who you are meant to be,
that you are worthy,
that you exist for yourself—
not for the eyes and opinions of others—
without the weight of judgment.
without morphing to fit expectations.
Resting in the now.
Celebrating who you are
now.

You are safe here in Art's embrace.

Girl Before a Mirror. Boisgeloup, March 1932. Oil on canvas, 64 x 51 ¼" (162.3 x 130.2 cm). Gift of Mrs. Simon Guggenheim. Picasso, Pablo (1881-1973) © ARS, NY Digital Image © The Museum of Modern Art/Licensed by SCALA / Art Resource, NY © 2023 Estate of Pablo Picasso/Artists Rights Society (ARS), New York Location: The Museum of Modern Art/New York, NY/U.S.A.

Girl Before a Mirror

Veiled in the mirror
My secret shame, but also
Sparks of truth, longing.

What happened when the Museum of Modern Art (MOMA) in New York City put all its rockstar artworks on tour in 2003? I became a groupie. Well, maybe not a groupie—after all I didn't follow the tour around the country or anything, but I did make the four-hour drive from Dallas to The Museum of Fine Arts Houston to see this blockbuster exhibit of MOMA masters, *Heroic Century: The Museum of Modern Art Masterpieces, 200 Paintings and Sculptures*. These were the works of art I repeatedly drooled over during my many years of education in art history: Monet's *Waterlilies*, Van Gogh's *The Starry Night*, Salvador Dalí's *The Persistence of Memory*, and art by Kandinsky, Marc Chagall, and more. I knew it would be an incredible experience, and I knew there was greatness waiting for me. What I didn't realize was that this museum visit would give me the most profound art experience of my life up to that point. This experience would change the direction and focus of my career and lead me through a decades-long journey out of my fractured pain and shame and into a place of peace and wholeness.

I was speechless as I ambled through the New Year's Day crowd from artwork to artwork. I progressed through the first rooms until I turned the corner into a new gallery. That's when Picasso's *Girl Before a Mirror* punched me in the gut. In absolute truth, I almost fell over when I saw her from across the room. Thankfully, this piece was not on the audio-guide tour, so few people stood before it. I weaved through the hordes of visitors as quickly as I could in order to see her up close. I was instantly brought to tears at the painting's sheer magnificence—huge, bold, and in your face. I couldn't take my eyes off the thick, rich colors and energetic lines—so composed yet so spontaneous and expressive.

This was not the first time I had such an emotional reaction to a work of art. I sobbed under Michelangelo's Sistine ceiling, sat on the floor stunned to tears near Donatello's *Mary Magdalene*, and clutched my heart as I looked up at the grandeur of Raphael's *School of Athens.* Hell, I cried all twelve times I saw *The Lion King* at the movie theater when I was in eighth grade. Rafiki holding up Simba at the end of "Circle of Life" is and always will be the most sublime moment in cinema. My tears often rest on the surface of my skin, but this reaction was bigger and more meaningful than any art experience before it. It was more significant than I could even explain at the time, and I have been unpacking and attempting to explain it ever since.

I was twenty-three years old, having recently completed my under-graduate degree in art history. Working as a part-time Gallery Teacher at the Amon Carter Museum of American Art in Fort Worth, I was applying for a Ph.D. in art history. From those tearful moments in the movie theater as a child to many awe-inspiring experiences seeing the Old Masters in Europe in college, art has always emotionally impacted me in unexplainable ways. I couldn't get enough of it. I didn't care when people told me an art history degree was useless or that I would be better off taking my intelligence into engineering to make more money. My heart and my soul needed art in ways that weren't clear to me then and that still reveal themselves to me on the regular twenty years later.

As I stared into the stark contrast of the blue and orange mirror frame of Picasso's painting, my mind started to wonder. I realized that what I was looking at was a mirror into my heart. This painting was so raw, deep, and pure; my reaction to it was equally visceral. Looking back, I see now that the painting took me out of my head and into my being—into my body, heart, and spirit. I became almost scared of it but mesmerized at the same time. Afraid of the feeling this painting provoked but also scared that if

I continued the study of art history, it would never come back. I vividly remember the dialogue going through my head, "If I stare at this painting long enough, it will lose this magic. If I take my eyes off it for a second, it won't be the same when I look again."

Standing in front of *Girl Before a Mirror*, I began to realize that I didn't want to deconstruct art and take away its essential meaning and feelings. I still don't want that. I realized that there was nothing I could learn about this painting or this artist that could have improved my experience of the artwork. Even now, I want to leave the mystery in the paintings themselves. I want to see the artworks for what they are and not for the analysis an art historian (who could have been me) pinned on them. At that moment, the viewing of this piece unlocked an inner knowing. As I stood before the *Girl*, I realized I wanted to let all the art I experience forge a collaboration with my heart, not just my head. Had I been more familiar with this particular painting, would I have reacted in such a way? If I knew more—about the particulars of the subject matter, that specific time frame in Picasso's life, or what he was thinking about the day he placed those aqua stripes on the *Girl*'s stomach—would it have still have knocked me off my feet?

What I realized that day was that art is magic. Art has the power to captivate, illustrate, and uncover hidden truths. Art can teach me lessons.

✳ ✳ ✳

 Shakespeare said that art is a mirror
held up to nature. And that's what it is.
The nature is your nature.
—Joseph Campbell in *The Power of Myth*

Art is not just art history or context. It is not just making or self-expression. It is not just lines and shapes and colors. It is not just the media it is made from. It's not just the artist or the culture.

✳ ✳ ✳

Art is *everything*. It is everything, yet it is nothing tangible.

Art is pure connection—from the artist to the viewer, from the viewer to themselves.

Art changes depending on who is looking and when they look. It is just for me in this moment, and then one second later, it is for you.

Art is magic. It is a shapeshifter. A hypnotist. An energy healer. It can cast spells. It can read minds and tell futures.

Art is a conjurer of ideas and emotions and change. A channeler of our deepest wants and needs. A container of memory. It can manipulate time or transport you to another time or dimension. Art can transmute a line into an image, into an idea, into a sensation, into an action.

Art is silent, still magic.

In this liminal space, I feared losing it and felt called to share it with everyone else. Captivated in the force field of *Girl Before a Mirror*, I looked around, wondering who else could be experiencing this magic...

Was I the only one?

How could something so drastic happen inside me while everyone else just goes about their business?

When you figure out a secret to life, how do you tell everyone about it?

What do you do when it's impossible to keep quiet?

On the four-hour drive home, I decided to ditch my Ph.D. applications and switch to studying art education instead of art history. I had been working as a museum educator since leaving college, and I knew now that my connection with art was not about getting *more* knowledge. It was about something deeper. I needed to spread the word. I needed everyone else to see what I saw and feel what I felt. I needed to lift the veil and tell the world this magic is real. I wanted everyone I came in contact with to step out above the daily grind and into themselves for just a minute to experience this sublime feeling. And I haven't stopped doing that in the almost twenty years since viewing this painting.

I've told this story repeatedly throughout my career, sharing this idea that art is more than its history, looking at art is deeper than appreciating it, and that you can discover things about yourself through your interactions with art. But rarely have I shared the other piece that happened that day in front of *Girl Before a Mirror*—a far more personal and intimate connection. That interaction was a catalyst for my career, nudging me in the direction that would someday lead to the creation of this book, but it was also a defining moment in my understanding of myself. When I saw that *Girl* standing in front of a mirror with her distorted, crying reflection, I saw myself and my own pain. I saw what I was trying to hide from and wept for the *Girl Before a Mirror* because she is me. At that moment, I was that *Girl*.

In the painting, a beautiful girl—blonde, blushed, shapely—grabs the sides of a mirror and stares thoughtfully into her reflection. What she sees in the mirror is not her actual, mirrored reflection but a disturbing, abstracted, deconstructed version of herself. The soothing pastel colors of the central figure turn to deeper blues, reds, and purples in her reflection. Her smooth lavender face becomes a deep, textured purple. Her formerly blushed cheeks with a boldly drawn eye now contain an empty black hole of an eye, dropping a thick orange tear. This painting was done in Picasso's iconic abstract, fractured, colorful style. Both figures are abstract nudes with rounded forms. Both remind me of a young girl who felt separate from the world around her—a girl whose insides don't match what is happening within.

She was me. I was her. We were the same, and I never had words for the feelings that this painting evoked until all at once, with this silent magic, I did.

✳ ✳ ✳

Growing up, I always felt like I didn't fit—an outsider looking in, not understanding why I felt so misunderstood, so out of place, so distant. I was an alien disguised as a human. I didn't understand social situations and got too wrapped up in emotions, feelings of judgment, and incredible self-consciousness. I was gifted, smart, and creative but a rule follower—a teacher's pet. My inner world was so deep and life-giving, but I didn't understand how to connect that inner world with the one outside where I was compelled to fit in. As a child, I spent a lot of time connecting with art and music, playing piano, drawing, and penning emotional poems about my sadness, love, and wonder about the world's mysteries. I had deep and overwhelming emotions that seemed to make everyone else uncomfortable, so I did what any gifted, smart, creative rule-follower would do—I locked them inside.

The deep purples, rich maroon, and saturated blues of the distorted reflection in the mirror of Picasso's painting remind me of this emotional place I once kept hidden inside my heart and body. These colors make me think of space now—zoomed-out views of galaxies and nebulas. Deep purple, one of my favorite colors, reminds me of mystical crystal balls and mysterious magic. If I gaze long enough into the depths of the dark purple, some hidden truth will reveal itself to me. When I saw this painting, though, I saw my tumultuous insides reflected back, not the incomprehensible beauty of galaxies or the delightful curiosity of mysticism. This emotional, closed-up part carried so much shame about who I was and how I never felt settled or whole. There was no beauty for me in those deep purples. Blinded by my dysmorphia, all I saw in her was my sadness and pain.

A mix of nature and nurture led me to this moment, to this feeling, to this painting. My neurodivergence and sensitivities make the world a little too loud and chaotic. Fabrics are too rough, noises are too jarring, and smells are too overpowering. Before I learned to set energetic boundaries, I was greatly influenced by the moods and emotional energy of the people around me. My undiagnosed ADHD created a natural yearning for novelty and adventure, so I threw myself into things I was excited about and hyper-focused on them without fear, but I couldn't seem to manage the day-to-day responsibilities of life—keeping my house clean, paying bills or sending birthday cards on time or even at all, or feeding myself. And although I lived with the repercussions of that chaos and sensitivity, when I was with *Girl Before a Mirror*, I wasn't yet consciously aware of these things about myself. In a way, those deep purples really did reflect back the mystery of who I was. Unknown and unseen, even by myself. All I knew then was that I didn't fit and something was wrong with me.

I am wrong. I am broken into pieces like Picasso's *Girl*.

These thoughts and beliefs don't exist in a vacuum. There is always a source. Childhood trauma played a significant role in my experience of life. My biological father was an alcoholic; my mom divorced him when I was five. I know little about those first five years, those precious pre-memory years before I started school, but what I do know of that time is chaos and instability. After the divorce, my mom remarried. My older sister and I saw my bio-dad for visitations until I was eight, when he just disappeared. His phone number was disconnected. He stopped calling. He left his job. He was gone.

I spent the next few years crying every night and writing sad poems about being abandoned. I was not told he was an alcoholic until many years later, so I subconsciously assumed the fault for his leaving, and as a consequence, I felt unloved and unlovable. Like many families, we didn't talk about our feelings much. I internalized my sadness as an inconvenience and a bother to others, and I learned to hide it the best I could. I'd guess most children of the '80s and '90s learned to stifle their emotions this way. After all, *Don't Worry Be Happy* hit number one on the Billboard charts in September 1988—the year before bio-dad's disappearance.

I've since learned that even though we don't have memories of our early childhood lives that we can explain with words, these experiences are still stored in our subconscious minds and in our bodies (Van der Kolk, 2015). Occasionally I wonder what little Cindy experienced during those rocky years. I've asked my sister about it. She's three years older than me and has an entirely different perspective. She remembers living in twelve houses and attending six elementary schools before age ten. This unstable and unpredictable environment undoubtedly made me feel profoundly unsafe as everyday chaos settled into my body.

This unstable black hole in my memory has given me a feeling of unease, knowing what I know now about what happened in my family during this time. I have an older brother I barely remember. I have flashes of memories. Broken glass and a drop of blood on a deflated balloon—a break-in, I think, at my bio-dad's job at an electronics store. I have bits and pieces of stories that won't ever be entirely told. Clinks of ice in my bio-dad's lowball glass, too big in his tiny apartment with the Cowboys playing in the background. Sitting in the middle of the bank seat of a pick-up truck singing loudly to "There's a Tear in My Beer." I have memories of saying goodbye to my bio-dad during the divorce, him crouching down, hugging me, and telling me he was leaving, but my mom says that never happened.

No matter how hard I try, I can't piece that time together into a cohesive memory. In the *Girl's* reflection in the mirror, she has a large dark green shape on her forehead, the location of her third eye—her intuition. Picasso only painted one eye on the reflection—a deep, mysterious plum purple. To me, these enigmatic dark spots on *Girl's* reflected face represent this blindspot in my memory and its impact on who I became in response—someone who never felt a sense of ease in her body and her surroundings, someone who felt untethered, someone who lost trust in her environment, in the ones who were supposed to love her, and in herself. Someone with a gaping hole.

Disconnected—
the *Girl Before a Mirror*
Makes a home for chaos and instability
She is in pieces and delicately assembled.
One breast floating—detached—away from her body,
her head balancing on a sharp point
without connection to a strong, solid, supportive neck.
Her body being p u l l e d in different directions—
her wholeness being ripped apart,
unable to find a grounded presence
in her body. She clutches the side of the mirror—
grasping tight to steady herself—
longing for something solid to ground her.

Having my father leave at such a young age, without the maturity and knowledge of the actual issues, caused me a deep fear of abandonment and immense sadness. Looking back at my elementary years, I see two Cindys, just as there are two *Girls* in the painting. There is the happy Cindy. Of course, there are joyful memories—the family vacations with long road trips, the boisterous Christmases, epic games of Uno™ and

Mexican Train Dominoes, the surprise gift of our beautiful Great Pyrenees dog (Sasha), and the neighborhood kid shenanigans. I remember the *Super Mario Bros. 3* marathons and seeing the shock and ridiculousness of Vanilla Ice for the first time on MTV® after school as my latch-key kid next-door neighbor friend and I ate ramen noodles and played "the floor is lava." I remember playing, crafting, painting, and watching Disney® animated movies on repeat. I remember my invention of "Do Something New Saturdays" and attempting (and failing) to paint the flowers from my mom's garden as my "something new." I remember playing school with the kids my mom watched in her home-based daycare—hearing those first whispers calling me to teach. But the first image I see and feel when I picture Cindy in elementary school is her crying in her room at night and the devastating feeling of being alone in that sadness.

I never felt safe sharing feelings in my household. Surely there were moments when my mom comforted me through the pain, but I don't remember them. What remains in my memory is loneliness. I remember creating a "student of the week" bulletin board for my fifth-grade class where I was supposed to show pictures of my family. I had many pictures of my bio-dad but no images of my stepdad. My mom told me it hurt my stepdad's feelings, and I remember crying as I removed my bio-dad's pictures from the board and added photos of my stepdad. As an adult, I totally understand where my mom was coming from. I see how that would affect my stepdad (now just "Dad"), but at the time, I learned that my pain, sorrow, and longing for my bio-dad were unacceptable. I learned that my feelings were a burden to other people. I learned that my feelings are less important than other people's. As a mother now, I can only imagine how lost my mom must have felt—how much pain she must have been in to see her child's pain and know that pain could not be fixed. Or rather, she couldn't fix it.

She was right. She couldn't fix my pain, so I carried the burden instead so she wouldn't have to. What's a child to do? Ignore the past. The past was over. Stay in the present, or better yet, look to the future. In the future, everything is fine, and we are all happy. I remember doing everything in my power to hide and control my feelings of loneliness and sadness. This was my burden—the sadness, anger, anxiety, and shame were problems I alone had to deal with.

Funny thing. When you hide something from the world, you also start to hide it from yourself. I didn't know how to process or feel my emotions because I was too busy hiding them. I didn't know how to get support for those problems, I didn't know that others felt the same way, and I just didn't know how to recover—how to ever feel like a whole person. I stuffed down all those feelings and kept them deeply buried.

I was working to build a thick and protective shell around myself—a physical, mental, and emotional armor that could hide it all. That armor protected the small, hurt me on the inside, the pained reflection of the *Girl Before a Mirror*, but it also functioned as armor to protect everyone else from seeing who I really was inside. I knew that they wouldn't like what they saw. I was drowning in my armor. The real me existed but only below the surface of inferiority, shame, fear, distrust, resentment, humiliation, and anxiety. These feelings were tearing at my insides while simultaneously pushing the wholeness of me away from the light, away from life.

With the trauma I experienced, I got the message that I was leavable and not good enough. So I threw myself into finding value and worthiness in some other way. (*My wholeness whispered to me even then, "you are worthy." I just didn't allow her to speak above a whisper, so I rarely heard her.*)

I learned I was naturally intelligent and creative, and being the best and brightest became my goal. I threw myself into being the most put-together, the most organized, and the most creative. I lived a life filled with competition. Competing with myself. Competing with my peers. Competing with my sister. I have to be the best because no one will leave me if I am the best. I must be beyond reproach.

My sadness eventually turned into fiery anger, into a hot-blooded "proving" energy. Committed to the story that my trauma only made me stronger, I continued reinforcing and building up my armor until it felt impenetrable —locking that fractured and distressed purple reflection deep inside.

If I am perfect, if I am smart,
I will be accepted, I will be loved, and no one will leave me.
My desire to be the best led to an incredible amount of ambition.
I will make something of myself.
I will prove that my trauma does not define me.
I will prove that I am lovable.
I will prove that I am good.
I will prove that I am worthy.
I will make others believe it.

❋ ❋ ❋

Control. It was all control. Control of myself to control how other people experience me. People couldn't be trusted to like me and stay unless I manipulated and controlled their experience of me. I learned to be hyper-attuned to other people's emotions. I learned to analyze and interpret every facial tic, body shift, or comment—adjusting my behavior accordingly. My mom (and, *hello*, all of American culture) was obsessed with diet and weight, so I learned to try to control my body as a way to connect with her and be acceptable in her eyes. I learned to control my emotions because feelings, even "good" ones, overwhelm people. If I overwhelm people, they will think I am too much, they will leave, and I will be alone.

In this perfectionism, I gripped tightly to that mirror just as *Girl* does, trying to control how people see her, all while knowing inside that she is not worthy. She is broken. She is wrong. She is unlovable. In this effort to control, I forced myself into ways of being that have taken decades to unravel and unlearn. Fractured and broken into pieces, I had to re-learn and remember how to be whole. After many years of dismantling my armor and finding my real reflection under all those layers of control, I can now easily see my story reflected in *Girl Before a Mirror*. But at age twenty-three in 2004, standing in front of Picasso's painting, most of these things, besides the obvious abandonment trauma, were still a mystery. When I stepped into that gallery in Houston, looking forward to the rockstar artworks that awaited me, I was chasing the wholeness deep inside of me. Somehow, even with all my armor, I knew I was still there and that this art could break through the armor, if only for a few moments, a few minutes, or if I was lucky a few hours. As I looked at the *Girl* in the mirror, I didn't know how to break free from the trap I continuously set for myself, but I heard the beginnings of a whisper that I could change the trajectory of my life.

What I know now is that I didn't fully know myself. I didn't understand the turmoil, suffering, intense social anxiety, and bouts of distracted depression and isolation. When I saw this *Girl* staring into her reflection in Picasso's painting, I saw myself in the mirror. I couldn't hide from it or distract myself from that pain. I saw who I am inside and out, and I felt a seed of something growing and shifting in me, and I knew art had something to do with it. I knew that art was starting to work its magic on me.

Something inside me has always known that art holds the answers for me, and that's why I do things like I did that day—driving eight hours roundtrip in one day to see an art exhibit. When I look at art, the world melts away. Time stops. The frantic pace of my ambition and overdoing slows. The pieces of my fractured, Picassoed insides find each other.

Art is about becoming whole. When I look at art, I know more about myself, the world, how to navigate emotions, and how to just exist as me without trying to control all aspects of myself and my environment. When I look at art, I feel less alone. I feel held. Understood by artists from across time and cultures, they see me—they always have—and I see them. Art became my best friend and my solace. My safety net. Art carried me through from that News Year's Day at the Museum of Fine Arts Houston to today as I write these words.

And *Girl Before a Mirror* held unknown secrets about me back in 2004. She was sending me messages and showing me the way. She taught me that my magic was my connection to art, and she invited me into the discovery of my own destiny. She was working her magic, helping me heal from my trauma and guiding me toward my most authentic self. She showed me my armor, mirrored my pain with her twisted purple insides, and sent me forward on my path to wholeness—a path illuminated by art.

self,

The Two Fridas

Compassionately
she sits with me, holds my hand,
her life blood, healing.

I was split into disparate pieces for much of my life. *Girl Before a Mirror* revealed two of these parts—the inner me filled with abandonment, sadness, and anger, and the outer me that holds it all in and tries to appear perfect. These various parts of me contradict—leaving me spinning and confused. Despite the inner turmoil, I contain a driving force more powerful than any trauma—a calling, an ambition, a zest for something bigger and grander than any normal life can hold. This ambitious side of me pulls my hesitant parts along, tirelessly pushing to expand and heal.

On one side, I have the instinct to hide, cower, and disappear, but the driven part does the opposite. She makes bold moves, starts businesses, dyes her hair purple, and travels the world, whether or not the rest of me feels ready. She whispers not unkindly to the melancholy parts, "It's time to heal; we have big shit to do. Let's fix this so we can move on." I've always known that my path would be forged by welcoming all the parts of me and coming to a place where I am whole instead of being split into pieces. Learning to be and accept all I am—from my inner child buried deep in my heart and then out to the edges of my humanity. This is the work.

I see my duality in another artwork I've always loved, *The Two Fridas* by Frida Kahlo. In this painting, two self-portraits of Frida sit together on a bench with navy and white storm clouds churning behind her. We can look at this painting and learn much about the life of Frida Kahlo; we can see her husband, Diego, in the picture in her hand and her broken heart. Her two clothing choices represent her dual heritage with her Mexican mother and her father of European descent. We can see her pain and discomfort in that stiff posture she lives with daily from the bus accident that caused her lifelong debilitating physical pain alongside the invisible pain of infertility. (Remember, I was going to be an art historian. One thing about knowing about the subject of a painting and the artists is that it sometimes brings you closer to our collective humanity.)

✳ ✳ ✳

Frida Kahlo painted her story with such heart and intensity that I can't help but find myself in her work. I like to think she would deeply understand my work because she knew what it was like to fervidly explore her own existence—painting around sixty self-portraits, a third of her known paintings (Chernick, 2020). I feel like her artwork was her own quest for wholeness, making sense of who she is, how she fits, how she feels, and what she experiences. When I find myself represented in her artwork, it doesn't diminish her story. It adds to it and to her legacy. Her art becomes a beacon for passionate people to find that soul connection that unites two people through art and stories.

Frida's art cuts straight into my heart. In her art, she embraces who she is on every level—in her uniqueness, her strangeness. Today, I relish in my strangeness—in what sets me apart. My deep inner, emotional experiences. My passion and my excitement. My capacity for radical wonder and deep conversation. My introversion and sensitivities. My desire for a slow evening with my feet dangling over the water, talking about big things with one person rather than dancing at a loud club with twenty. My ability to pick up on the slightest of emotions from just about anyone and the ability to just know things about people without having to be told. These things that I have now come to know about myself as being major positives in my life—things that make me who and why I am—once made me feel alienated, misunderstood, and ashamed. When I was younger, in my late teens and twenties, I felt hopelessly and utterly alone in this strangeness.

Looking at *The Two Fridas*, I wonder if the first Frida (on the left) felt like this, sitting primly in a white, lacy dress with a stiff collar up to her chin, puffy sleeves, and red embroidered flowers along the ruffled bottom hem. Above her left breast, her heart sits outside her body. The dress around the heart dissolves or is torn away, revealing the skin underneath. The heart is open, but not in a good way—showing white structures inside, which I imagine shouldn't be visible in a healthy heart. Veins come from the heart down to her right hand, where she holds a surgical clamp to stop blood dripping from the vein onto her pristine, white dress. Other veins flow directly from her heart to her second self's heart, which is whole, healthier looking, and brighter.

The second Frida wears a gold, blue, and olive green dress, more typical of the Mexican artist's iconic colorful style. She holds a small picture of her husband, Diego Rivera, in her left hand as veins wrap around her arm and into her whole, red heart, continuing to the heart of the first Frida. Besides the clothes and the heart's health, there are more subtle differences between the two Fridas. The first Frida's skin is paler and takes on a slightly sickly tone. Her posture is more upright—sitting in a way that looks uncomfortable and forced. My sensitivities prickle when I look at Frida on the left; the dress seems itchy, constricting, and musty, the posture looks painful, and her heart seems to burn in distress. Her open, dripping vein and washed-out skin make me feel light-headed and cold. Although the facial expressions are nearly identical (Kahlo's classic serious stare), I sense pain and discomfort behind the face of the first Frida. However, her counterpoint seems at ease and comfortable with her pelvis shifting forward and a relaxed curve to her posture. Her red beating heart fills her with a warm, vital glow.

My value was built
on the fickle foundation of
interpreted comments
and over-analyzed expectations
With shame as the mortar

between not acceptable

and not enough

With a body to shrink,

Thoughts to silence,

Shyness to quash,

Emotions to suppress,

Wonder to quell,

In the depths of my pain,

I desperately wanted to be loved

But I didn't even like who I was

because I was not
perfect
But...

The glue that unites the whole

I longed to know love.

I longed to feel valuable.

I longed to take up space.

I longed to feel heard.

I longed to be seen.

I longed to be witnessed.

I longed for vitality.

I longed for comfort.

in the warmth of my skin

at home within myself

What if...
the only true perfection is being
perfectly
me.

I really thought there was no way that anyone could ever like me because I had proof that I drove away a parent, one of the people who was supposed to love me the most, who was always supposed to be there.

I knew I was different because I had an example in my own house of what I perceived to be perfect. I have an older sister, Jenny, who was so cool, so funny, so bright, so talented, so talkative, so seemingly confident, so delightfully quirky, and so extroverted. She has her own story of our trauma and how that made her the way she is. I know that my experience of her may or may not reflect how she felt about herself on the inside, but what I saw as a child was someone I desperately wanted to be like but who I was nothing like. I didn't know what made me different, but I knew I wasn't like her. And it wasn't even like I just wanted to be like her; I felt like I should be like her. That I was broken if I wasn't like her. I felt like an embarrassment to her and my parents because I wasn't like her. And it didn't help that we were sisters—with the nitpicking and controlling big sisters tend to do, especially when they feel responsibility tugging at them. Comments that undoubtedly came from a helpful place within her immediately became misinterpreted and internalized into shame and not enough-ness for me.

And her bangs were so fluffy and so amazing. I could never get my limp, lifeless bangs to look like hers.

> **66** I squat there and think about how you get trained early on as a woman to perceive how others are perceiving you, at the great expense of what you yourself are feeling about them. Sometimes you mix the two up in a terrible tangle that's hard to unravel. **99**
>
> — Lily King in *Writers & Lovers*

And, of course, being different when you are young means being an outcast. It means having no friends and not belonging with family, so I did all I could to pretend that I wasn't as different as I felt. I could feel myself bending into the first Frida's ideal to please and fit. But the problem is that I am not a good actor or liar. My desire to pretend I am someone I am not clashes with the inner knowing that I cannot possibly do that without revealing who I am trying to hide. This combination further blended with a natural inclination towards introversion and shyness that led me to completely clam up, turn deep inside myself, and hide from the world. Every social situation became the intricate act of diffusing a bomb or perhaps an open heart surgery, as reflected in The Two Fridas, where each wire, vein, or conversation thread became a threat that could blow up, bleed out, or reveal to everyone that all was not as it seemed with me. Just a slip of the first Frida's hands would release the pressure of that surgical clamp, letting the blood flow from the open vein.

I can see this Cindy—trying to play the perfect part and trying to fit in—in The Two Fridas. Like the Frida on the left, I made it my mission to hold it together—trying to appear like everything is okay. But it's easy to see that the first Frida is struggling—her heart is not fully pumping the blood she needs, and her body is hurting, as seen by her stiff posture. Her clothes are not the ones she is comfortable in; her skin pales as the blood pumps away from her body. It takes all of her energy to hold it together. Her thoughts and feelings are all directed toward the challenge of just existing.

There is nothing left for joy, nothing left for love, nothing left for peace, nothing left for finding wholeness.

What developed slowly throughout my childhood and adolescence and then raged in my twenties were layers of shame upon shame upon shame upon shame. One of the biggest ahas from my years of therapy in my twenties was when I first recognized and named that shame. As innocuous as it sounds now, I had been talking to my therapist about how much judgment I would place on myself for drinking Gatorade® of all things. I wouldn't let anyone see me drink a Gatorade® because I thought they would think that I believed that Gatorade® was healthy to drink even though I knew it was just sugar and that water was better and Gatorade® was just hype. That Gatorade® I wanted to drink represented my failure at health. That Gatorade® was why I was fat. That Gatorade® was a threat to other people's view of how smart I was. And then not only am I judging myself for drinking the Gatorade®, judging others for their perceived judgment of my Gatorade®, but then I am judging myself for judging myself about the Gatorade®. It's a never-ending judgment spiral that didn't just stop there. My therapist asked what I thought was underneath the drama about Gatorade®, and the word shame came to mind. I remember immediately feeling stunned by the word and its implications.

The undeniable truth of that word.
Shame.

Once I recognized that shame was beneath the Gatorade® spiral, I started to view all of my actions and experiences through this lens of shame. Brené Brown (2013), a leading shame researcher and author, defines shame as "the intensely painful feeling or experience of believing that we are flawed and therefore unworthy of love, belonging, and connection." I sincerely wanted to be loved and to belong, as we all do at our very human cores, but I also believed deep down that I was not worthy of that love and belonging. I was too much, too controlling, too emotional, too rough around the edges, too boring, and too burdensome. And like the dark and stormy clouds behind *The Two Fridas*, shame created a cloud between who I thought I should be and who I actually was. It obscured my vitality, my aliveness. It hid away the things that set me apart from others—the things that truly lit me up and brought me the most joy.

As I have healed over the last twenty years from this shame, it has felt like unburying the real me. I always knew she was there. I always knew there was a vitality within me that no one could see, that I couldn't really access, but it was there, pushing me along with ambition and adventure. That inner knowing made excavating the layers of shame, one painful layer at a time, worth it. I knew it was there because I saw occasional glimmers of what was underneath. The dense cloud of shame occasionally parted—just as the clouds behind *The Two Fridas* seem to move and churn—and revealed who I was underneath it all. And when those clouds separated long enough for me to fully embody her, it was sublime. It was taking a big clean breath of air. It was red, oxygenated blood pumping through my healthy heart. It was the comfort of a relaxed posture and a warm embrace. It was my exterior matching my interior. It was wholeness.

In my senior year of college, I had a moment where this real me peeked out from behind the shame cloud. My college years were not the cliched "best years of my life." My college years were mostly spent on my landline phone with my long-distance boyfriend (now husband) or alone in my apartment in an old hand-me-down recliner, watching reruns of Friends, playing Boggle® on my clunker early-aughts laptop, with my only friend, Boo (my sweet black cat), curled up on my legs. There were no parties or late-night study sessions. Any friends I made were short-lived or situational.

This glimmer of the real me came during my class, *Medici Florence and the Politics of Art*, taught by my favorite art history professor, Dr. Louis Waldman, at the University of Texas at Austin. To me, he was the epitome of a good teacher. So passionate and animated, he made Renaissance art exciting and intriguing. And even though it was never really a favorite art movement of mine, he captivated me with his teaching style. I saw my own passion for art in his enthusiastic tirades—standing up on the tables with his personality lighting up the dark lecture hall as he waved his hands around in excitement, talking about what I loved most—art. He loved what I loved and made it come alive, drawing me to his classes.

As we were preparing for a test in class one day, he invited students to the podium to lead the test review (a teaching strategy I adopted later in my career). I can't remember if I was randomly selected or if I volunteered. Still, for a spell, I clicked through the slides of the Botticellis, Bronzinos, and Brunelleschis in front of the class, asking my peers questions about the content for the exam. This shy girl, who probably had never talked to anyone in that class before, stood at the front of the room and became entirely herself for a few minutes. Had I been told to converse with anyone in that room, I would have flailed in my anxiety and self-consciousness, but standing in front of the class, I became something that had been quietly whispering to me for a while. I became a teacher.

Later that day, Dr. Waldman approached me while studying in the art building and said, "Cindy, you are a natural-born teacher." Not only had I felt it in front of the class, but it was noticed by someone I admire. That comment pierced through the dense cloud of shame and became a moment I have always remembered. From that point on, this is what I knew to be true. I am a teacher. And I am not just a teacher but a damn good teacher. Tears spring to my eyes, and goosebumps percolate on my arms as I write these words today—twenty-one years later. A quick comment to a shy student can send ripples through the rest of their life. It's powerful.

Teaching gave me a feeling of connection, of belonging, of love. The feeling of being the right person at the right time doing the right work. The sense of alignment and flow. So I chased those feelings as I continued to teach as often as I had the chance in my college internships and then in art museums and later in community colleges and public schools, and then in my business, Art Class Curator, helping other teachers love the craft of teaching with works of art. I would come alive as soon as I got in front of a group of kids or adults. I used to think that my change in demeanor was because teaching was a type of performance. It was putting on a show, embodying a character, and pretending to be confident—faking it until I made it. But I realized along the way that this confidence wasn't an act. As I started to see the results of my teaching with the connections my students made, I realized that I really am a natural-born teacher. I'm good at this.

> **66** Teaching is like photosynthesis: making food from air and light. It tilts the prospects for life a little. For me, the best class sessions are right up there with lying in the sun, listening to bluegrass, or swimming in a mountain stream. **99**
> — Richard Powers in *Bewilderment*

In my teaching, I could feel the full fire of my passion for art and share it with others. I could make a real impact on people. And with that confidence and knowledge, hidden parts of my personality could emerge. When teaching, I could allow myself to be charming, funny, and approachable. I could be excited and passionate without abandon and without the fear of overwhelming people. I was safe with the art. I was allowed to marvel and celebrate the delightful without dodging judgment or shame. I experienced firsthand how Dr. Waldman's enthusiasm penetrated his classrooms, so I let my natural enthusiasm emerge. Teaching allowed me to feel whole.

✳ ✳ ✳

This revelation of spirit, this eye in the storm of my shame, began to open up some big, unanswered questions. How can I be a passionate and effervescent teacher while being riddled with shame and social anxiety the rest of the time? How can I be the vital and at ease Frida on the right while also feeling the intense pain and discomfort of the left Frida? How could I relish in the joy of the teaching moment while also wanting to hide and sometimes just cease to exist? Because as delightful as that break in the shame cloud was, the rest of the time, I was not okay and didn't know why or how to help myself feel better.

The year that Dr. Waldman proclaimed me a "natural born teacher" was the very same year that my anxiety and shame overwhelmed me to the point of failing my advanced Italian class, not because I didn't know the content but because I couldn't even open the door to the building to go to class. I can still feel the panic that set in as I reached for the door handle. I felt electric jolts up and down my limbs in that intense fight, flight, or freeze moment. I have to shake out my arms as I write, just with the memory of them. These drastic physiological responses stopped me from attending class and sent me fleeing—crying on the bus ride home.

Every inch of my body would not allow me to enter that building. Every inch of my body told me that I was in danger. I didn't understand what was happening. It felt so much bigger than just not wanting to go to class. I couldn't breathe at the thought of even walking in that door. I didn't understand how someone who spent her whole life priding herself on being a straight-A student and being perfect could have taken a fall quite so hard. I knew that, socially and emotionally, I was a mess but that I could do no wrong academically. This class tore apart that identity. I really didn't understand what was happening to me. I know now I had a nervous system response, but at the time, I didn't understand what was happening in my body that wouldn't let me into the classroom. I didn't yet even know that anxiety disorders existed.

Not only did I fail that class in the last semester of my senior year, but I also failed to officially graduate on time because of it. My self-esteem was so low, my confidence was so shaken, and my shame was so deep that I allowed my whole family to come down and celebrate my college graduation. I walked across that stage and didn't have a degree on the other side of that handshake because I had failed my last class. I've never told my family this, and this is probably the first time they are learning it, reading this book. Sorry, Mom, I lied.[1]

Not only was I leaving behind "the best years of my life" with no friends or stories to tell, but I drove away from college with no degree, which called into question my whole identity and white-knuckled title as the most intelligent person in the room. Wholly shaken and at what felt like rock bottom, I started to seek answers. This was in 2002, and the internet was still very young and not as it is today. Social media didn't yet exist, and no brave and vulnerable influencers normalized mental health struggles. It wasn't easy to find answers unless you knew exactly what you were looking for, especially when you had never even heard of the concept of anxiety disorders. What I did end up finding were books at the library about Social Anxiety Disorder and Adult Children of Alcoholics.

Opening these books, I had never felt so seen and understood.

My fear of going to the same restaurant two days in a row because I didn't want the same person to take my order and think that I was such a gross person that I would eat fried chicken more than once a week.

My complete inability to answer the phone.

My hiding in fear in the hallway (because it has no windows) when someone knocked on my door.

My going out of my way to avoid even walking by people at the grocery store.

My feelings of terror of that damn Italian class.

My deep fears of abandonment.

My overactive sense of control and responsibility.

My stuffing down of all feelings, positive or negative.

Suddenly, all of those things became symptoms.

Suddenly it became not that I am broken beyond repair, that I am unloved, that I don't belong. Suddenly it became a thing that was real—a tangible thing with a name. Something I could treat. Something I could work to overcome that would lead to me feeling better.

And while the awareness of the problem's existence doesn't immediately fix its impact, at least now I had a place to start. I took the discovery of these books as proof that the real Cindy was there underneath it all,

[1] Don't worry, Mom. I did end up retaking the class at a different university and graduating the next year.

holding my hand like Frida, sending me her lifeblood, and pulling me forward along my path to healing with her sweet and caring presence.

All I needed
to do was to help those shame clouds move along
and let the sun shine through.
All of my energy from that point on
focused on how to feel better.
All I needed
to do was hold my own hand
with slow, gentle compassion.

Claude Monet, *Water Lily Pond*, 1900. The Art Institute of Chicago

Water Lily Pond

Up close or away,
I can just see what I see.
The truth, elusive.

The difference between me and a Monet painting...
the artwork is not trying to be something it is not.
It is not trying to hide the mess within.
It is not judging itself for being less polished and finished than its counterparts
from more refined art movements.
It does not care if some people don't like it or "get" it.
The painting is
whole in its messiness,
whole in its presence.

While writing this book, when I've shared bits and pieces of my writing,
I've gotten comments from people from my past. They didn't see it. They
didn't see my awkwardness, extreme discomfort, or lack of fitting in.

They didn't see *IT*. The *IT* I anxiously and constantly fretted over wasn't something they perceived.

Now, while I am sure many people did see *IT*, these are not the people I heard from when I shared my voice. A few of these people were surprised to hear of my struggles with anxiety and shame when what they saw was a passionate and accomplished person. These unfathomable comments stunned me and made me realize how deep that divide is between what you notice about a person and what is happening with them on the inside. There is so much we don't know, and there is so much we assume.

Look at the art of Claude Monet. An Impressionist, Monet paints quickly—trying to capture the light and the essence of a place outside *en plein air*. Standing across the room, the paintings look realistic, but as soon as you get close up, you see all of his quick and messy brushstrokes in completely unexpected colors.

> 66 She's a full-on Monet.
> It's like a painting, see.
> From far away it's okay,
> but up close it's a big ol' mess. 99
> — Cher in the movie *Clueless*

The metaphor is obvious. We are all way more messy and complicated than we appear from the outside, but Monet's paintings have an even deeper layer of complexity than what is traditionally known.

I visited Monet's home and gardens a few years ago in the beautiful village of Giverny, an hour or so outside of Paris. I was dumbfounded walking through the expansiveness of Monet's intricately-composed yet wild gardens with nearly one hundred types of trees, plants, and flowers. It was like stepping into his paintings, and as I meandered through, the vistas seemed to morph into and out of works of art. His gardens were curated to perfection—each plant a choice based on color and intuition, an art unto itself. And while I've never been the biggest fan of Impressionism in general, I was stunned by the experience and haven't looked at his paintings the same way since—how many of his paintings are not actually even just quick paintings as I once thought. When you factor in the gardening, they are composed twice, once as a garden and second as a painting.

Unless you've walked through those gardens and spent time with the paintings in person, you don't truly know them, and even then, you only know your experience of them. And even then, the light on the day you visited the garden was different than the day Monet painted that exact spot. Impressionists taught us that lighting is everything. And as it turns out, perception isn't everything. I always welcome a reminder that what I make up about other people and their perceptions of me is not always the truth.

Chantal Joffe, *Self-Portrait Naked with My Mother II*, 2020.
Oil on board, 243 x 181.5 cm (95 ⅝ x 71 ½ in) © Chantal Joffe.
Courtesy of the artist and Victoria Miro

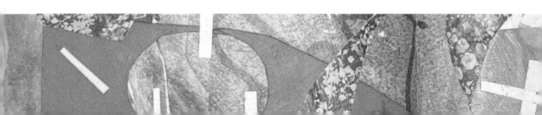

Self-Portrait Naked with My Mother II

We started as one—
My body mixed with your mind.
I am now my own.

I first learned I was "fat" when I was ten.[2] A blonde boy named Michael told me, "You have a big butt." I already stood out as the tallest girl in class with my larger, big-boned structure—always standing top left in class pictures—but the size of my butt? This was news to me. At home later that day, combing through the family photo albums to corroborate his claim, I found a picture of me baking with my Nana. The picture was taken from behind as I cookie-cuttered our annual batch of Christmas cookies at my Nana's vinyl-covered kitchen table, with my white t-shirt stretched over my clearly oversized backside—adding a filter of shame to this lovely family memory.

A heaviness set in as I reached behind and felt my flesh with curiosity. A new and unfamiliar burden made itself present—an awareness that my

---

[2] Content warning for my fellow readers who are also recovering from the impact of diet culture. This chapter is not about my "weight journey," but about how I traveled from a place of shame around my body to a place of peace with a deeper understanding of my body as it is.

body means something to other people and that there was inherent judgment in Michael's comment, whether or not he intended to be critical. The size and appearance of my body were no longer just facts; my body was offensive. It took up too much space. It bothered Michael. And so began my long and tortured relationship with my body.

❋ ❋ ❋

Like nearly all women who grew up in the eighties, nineties, and early aughts in America, diet culture had a death grip on our society's hearts, minds, bodies, and souls, particularly of our mothers. Any woman who is just one size above a size six or five pounds above a randomly set "ideal weight" seems to have some version of the same story—the lunches our mothers packed for us with half of a sandwich with the crusts cut off and three strawberries, the Buns of Steel® workout videos (gotta "squeeze those cheeseburgers out of those hips!"), the arbitrary demonization of perfectly-fine foods like fruit, butter, bread, and eggs, and the shameful dressing room arguments when clothes didn't fit right because it was our fault for not having bodies that conform. I don't know that it ever entered anyone's mind (certainly not mine) to question that perhaps that particular article of clothing was not the proper cut for our shapely forms. We thought we had to change our bodies to fit the clothes instead of changing the clothes to fit our bodies.

As I gained more and more weight in my teen years and early adulthood, my shame about my weight added more and more pressure onto my spirit, which was already burdened with crippling anxiety and pent-up sadness and anger from my childhood. My large size and inability to control it intensified that shame. And it didn't help that because my size is a physical trait, I couldn't hide it like I could everything else. I had to wear and display my shame to everyone I met. My fat body is the first thing you notice, and there is no escaping how our human nature naturally trains us to look for and see differences. Our brains are wired to look for anomalies, to other, to find the thing that does not fit.

When I pulled up to the grocery store, in my car with the seat all the way back with the seat belt extender stretched across my ample body, I would freeze in fear if there were any groups of people idly waiting by the door.

I would wait for them to disperse before I dared walk into the store to avoid catching their knowing nods, under-the-breath comments, or furtive glances at their feet to avoid eye contact. Because although I know some of these interpretations were made up in my head about these random strangers, there's a lot of truth to that judgment. I myself immediately notice someone's size as much as I hate it, and fat jokes are still rampant in television and movies—one of the last groups of people it is still socially acceptable to mock publicly. And we watch an estimated forty-five million Americans go on diets yearly just so they won't look like us (Searing, 2018).

As fat people, we wear our size as a badge for everyone to see, like a Scarlet Letter, and society has taught us that we should be ashamed of it. So most of us are. This familiar body shame made me gasp when I saw the painting *Self-Portrait Naked with My Mother II* (2020) by Chantal Joffe at the *Women Painting Women* exhibit at The Modern Art Museum of Fort Worth (Karnes, 2022). In this painting, the nude artist sits close together on a sofa with her clothed mother. They both sit with their legs crossed at the ankles. The artist's hands are on her knees, and the mother rests one elbow on her knees and the other on the arm of the sofa—leaning away from her daughter. Sitting shoulder to shoulder, both women gaze uncomfortably to their right. Although they both have severe expressions on their faces, the emotions of each are different and palpable. It's uncomfortable to witness them together like this. I know how this situation feels and don't want to relive those feelings as I look.

The artist looks to be dissociating from the scene and leaving her body—her eyes seem vacant, somewhere else entirely. Her body is slumped as if trying to make herself small. She appears to be bracing herself for the inevitable judgment coming her way—whether it is a direct comment, a passive-aggressive remark, or just her inner critic interpreting every move or comment of her mother as judgment regardless of the intent. Knowing it is coming and preparing for the impact causes her to not be fully present with her mother, fully present with herself, and not be fully in her body. I get the sense that she would float away from her body if possible—that she would do anything to leave this meat suit behind and go to a happier place for a little while.

A note: I talk about my mother in this chapter, especially regarding her relationship with dieting and diet culture as I perceived it growing up. I love my mom, and although I may have had some blame or mild resentment in the past towards her, I don't feel that way today. What I talk about today are reasons, not blame. Just like I am a product of my own environment, upbringing, societal and cultural norms, and trauma, she also has her own garden of influences and complexities that led her to the choices that were best for her at the time. I don't write about her to blame or judge her but simply to provide context and a backdrop to my healing and journey to wholeness.

I interpret art through many of the same processes and thoughts that happen when I interpret another person. My trauma and natural sensitivities trained me to pick up on other people's emotions and analyze their actions. With enough time, too, I've learned I can often trust the assumptions I make about other people, but I recognize that they are indeed assumptions, and I need to remember that my interpretations may not line up with someone's truth.

When I look at an artwork, I can't help but put myself into it—to find my place in the art. And in this painting, I am the naked artist, sitting vulnerably next to her seemingly-critical mother. My interpretations of the artworks in this book are 100 percent my own. I am not presuming to know the pain or internal world of the artist, just as I am not presuming to understand my mother's pain or inner world. I have theories, of course, but the artist hasn't told me what she thinks besides providing me this image to ponder, just as my mom keeps the stories of her past and her emotions about them locked in tightly. She doesn't talk about her history. Like at all. Ever. I long to really know her, but I have come to terms with the fact that I probably never will know her as well as I want to. It is her choice to share that with me, and so far, my mom's stories remain untold.

" This is the thing about people...
You can look at a person and truly have
no idea what they are holding inside. "
— Charmaine Wilkerson in *Black Cake*

❋ ❋ ❋

The artist and her mother sit arm to arm but have very closed-off body language with their ankles and arms crossed. They are physically touching, but I can't help but notice the significant gaps between them—unsaid things and unexpressed emotions. I can feel from the image of the artist a desire to be seen, truly seen, and loved without reservation, without criticism—unconditionally accepted with a yearning for belonging. Her nakedness shows that vulnerability and that longing. Even the artist's use of the word naked instead of nude in the title indicates that it's more than a lack of clothing on the body. We use "nude" when we celebrate the body and its beauty. We use "nude" to celebrate our sensuality and our curves. We use "naked" when the body becomes something raw, something to be consumed and judged, something uncomfortable, or the form in which we feel the most vulnerable, like when an infant emerges from the mother's womb—sticky and crying, the state we are when we stand in front of the mirror noting our "flaws." Nude is beautiful but naked feels supremely uncomfortable.

And I deeply feel this sense of vulnerability about my body as I sit next to my own mother. For as long as I can remember, my mom has been obsessed with all things weight. Every food she or others eat is a value judgment—good or bad. Her own size and the size of others are up for scrutiny and commentary. The shame stemming from boys (like the big-butt-shaming Michael) or strangers that I walk by on the way into the grocery store or anyone else pales in comparison to the shame I used to feel in the presence of my mother in a body two or sometimes three times the size of hers. Because a part of me knew that even though she loved me more than anything, even though she would do anything for me. I knew I could trust in her for anything I would ever need, even though she would jump in the car and drive across the big state of Texas at a moment's notice to be with me when I broke a bone, that I—in many ways—was a failure. Yes, I felt like a failure to myself, but to be a failure to my mother somehow has a more painful sting. And I inherently knew that it wasn't just my failure; she probably believed that somehow my size was her failure as a mother. And that is the elephant in the room when I am with her.

* * *

As I look at this painting, it intrigues me to think about the connection of our bodies to those of our mothers. We were created from our mothers. We were cells in their wombs when they were in their own mothers. We were once a part of their bodies, and growing up is a process of separating ourselves from our mothers. How do we go from our mothers pinching our cheeks, kissing our heads, squeezing our little baby thighs, and delighting in our scent to our mothers scrutinizing our bodies, analyzing everything we do with our bodies, and making our bodies about their success or failure as parents? As this process of separating ourselves and our bodies from our mothers' bodies happens, the physical connection no longer exists, but the emotional and psychological connection still remains. The remnants are part of the tension between Joffe's naked self-portrait and the painting of her mother. In this painting and in any mother-child relationship, there are a lifetime of stories, of conversations, of tension, of love, of vulnerability, of the daughter and the mother constantly feeling that disconnect and that tug to better know each other but also still be individuals—of always having that sometimes painful understanding that once we were together and now we are apart.

Once, we were one, and now we are two.

Looking at the painting, I see the whole being of the artist, and I think even if I didn't know the title, I would have known that the naked woman was the artist—she seems real, known, and understood. But I can't look at the mother without seeing a bit of a caricature, a facade. The woman in this painting only represents the physical likeness of the artist's mother captured through the biased lens of the artist. This likeness is not the complex woman that her mother undoubtedly is. And I experience my mother the same way. I know her from the perspective of daughter to mother only. I see her obsession with dieting, and I have felt the significant impact of it throughout my life, but I don't get to truly understand how that part of who she is came to be. Any amount of psychoanalysis on my part can make up stories about who she is deep down and how she feels, but I don't get to witness the complexity of who she really is from the inside.

From the outside looking in, I see a mother who raised her children in a generation unlike the more accepting and open one my own daughters are growing up in.

Mom, who had her own issues with her mother and the absence of her father, who traveled for work many months out of the year.

Mom, who lived within the strict confines of a patriarchy that said your worth was determined by your looks alone.

Mom, who got the message that women should be seen and not heard, learned that to get by as a woman, you must fit into a perfect mold and make yourself immune to criticism.

Mom, who escaped a marriage with a raging alcoholic without a cent to her name and then raised her two young daughters to be both ambitious and highly successful women and amazing mothers themselves.

Mom, who fought like hell to keep her daughters safe and thriving in a world that wasn't built for strong-willed, creative daughters who have something to say and who break the mold of what a woman "should" be.

Mom, who makes the choice to focus on the present and the future instead of rehashing and feeling the pain of the past.

When I look at the artist's mother in the painting, her facial expression is tightlipped and downturned. Sorry to Chantal Joffe's mom, but this woman seems super grumpy. My mom, on the other hand, is the opposite of grumpy. Although I feel like "negative" or uncomfortable emotions were not tolerated in my life growing up, there is something to be said about my mother's expression of happiness. She chooses happiness every day. She deliberately smiles when answering the phone so that you can hear it in her voice. I can hear her singsong "Hello!" so clearly in my head. She doesn't talk about her painful past and chooses to focus on the present.

When I hold up the artist's mother to my own (yes, I am making a little comparison here), I imagine that although my mother's happiness is omnipresent, it also most certainly covers the same type of pain and suffering that I see in the artist's mother—at least at times. My mother is human, just like the rest of us. I know that some of her suffering existed because she thought she needed to bend and change to be accepted and get by. And as a mother, you have an incessant need to figure this life out because you have these children who depend on you, looking to you to make sense of the world and feel safe. When it isn't safe, mothers need to find a way to control the variables to make it safer and survivable.

Looking back now, I realize I didn't know another way to interact or be with myself and my mother—none of us knew any other way growing up in our context. I always viewed my weight as the cause of so many of my burdened feelings. So when I went for a new round of therapy in my late twenties to "for once and for all" get to the bottom of my weight issues (society has taught us that our weight is because of a flaw or broken part deep within us after all), I was shocked that after months of therapy, I arrived at a new and actually quite scary place. What if I could feel light, happy, and free and still be fat? What if, like my mother, I choose happiness, but unlike my mother, choose to love my body as it is? What if yo-yo dieting and self-shaming were the problems and not the solutions? What if my happiness was not derived from the approval of my physical appearance by my mother, sister, fifth-grade Michael, or random strangers I happened to be walking by but by how I felt about myself on the inside? What if I could put down the weapons of control—the calorie counting apps, the scales, the measuring tape, the fat bombs, the Snackwell®'s cookies—and pick up new tools that work with and for my body rather than against it? What if I took the time and energy I wasted trying to fit my body into society's impossible standards and used it to live the joyful and zestful life I was waiting to live once I lost weight?

> **I wasn't intrinsically without value, I was just doomed to live in a culture that hated me. For me, the process of embodying confidence was less about convincing myself of my own worth and more about rejecting and unlearning what society had hammered into me.**
> — Lindy West in *Shrill: Notes From a Loud Woman*

What if my size is not my or my mother's failure but society's failure to provide a safe and accepting world for women to flourish? Joffe's mother, my mother, and thousands of other women have spent billions of dollars trying to fix something that is not broken. Women spend all of their emotional energy trying to control their bodies and also trying to control their daughters' bodies, and for what? We think it is so we can feel like we belong, that we can be loved, and that we won't be alone. Still, it is so blonde boys named Michael who grow up to be white men in power feel more comfortable in our presence, so systems of patriarchy and white supremacy can remain intact.

* * *

When did I stop trusting my body?
Why did I start trying to control it?
Who taught me that I know better than my own lungs how to breathe?
My lungs

    e x p a n d

    collapse

    e x p a n d

    collapse

    transporting

    the breath of life

Who taught me that I know better than my own heart how to beat?
My heart

    ba boom

    ba boom

    ba boom

    rhythmically, repeatedly,

    intuitively knowing to adapt

    and send its electric pulse

    reaching out for connection

    and coherence

Who taught me that I know better than my own hunger?
My hunger

    churning

    growling

    signaling my need

    for energy

Who taught me to push past my body's limits?
My body

    resetting with sleep

    allowing itself to rest

    unapologetically

Who taught me to stop trusting what my body feels?
My body

    feeling

    fear when its safety is threatened

sadness when it's lost something important

awe in the face of beauty

Who taught me that my body is for anyone other than me?

My body

    not needing

    to be reigned in

    to be made small

    to be made beautiful

Who taught me that my body was not already perfect?

    that my size and features are beautiful and hearty,

    that my heart and lungs aren't strong,

    that my feelings aren't valid?

My body

    instinctively

    supporting

    thriving

    knowing

    teaching

What if I started

listening to my body?

* * *

With some therapy and this inkling that maybe dieting is not the answer to my life's happiness (who'd have thought?), I trusted my body enough to have my first baby. And It. Was. Miraculous.

I was at war with my body for twenty-eight years, and then it went and created a whole brand new person. Among other things, it made an entirely new organ to grow that new person, rearranged my insides, raised my heart and breathing rates to support the creation of the baby, increased my total blood volume, and even created a perfect food source for the baby. I didn't have to tell it to do any of that. It knew what to do and when to do it. I didn't have to control any part of that process, yet in the end, a beautiful and whole daughter arrived. And in an instant, I, too, was someone's mother.

I became a mother with my own naked daughter screaming next to me. Throughout my life up until this point, my relationship with my body has been in many ways about my mother. She was blamed for it. I was ashamed of it. Now that I realize we have separate bodies and identities, I know I can have my own relationship with my body. My body can be for me and not for anyone else. We once were one, and her impact is in every part of me, but now I can choose, and I recognize that choice.

I can break the cycle and start a new story of my body.

I can learn about my body.

I can discover what my body wants and needs.

I can notice how my body reacts.

I can work with it rather than against it.

I can stop fighting my body and let it be fully for me.

I can celebrate what my body allows me to do.

I can trust in the knowledge and insight it holds.

And I can learn to trust in the authority and sovereignty of my own daughters' bodies, stifling that motherly desire to fix all of their "problems"—knowing that their existence is already my success and that whoever they become is success if they are allowed to be their authentic selves. My highest wish as their mother is for them to learn to trust themselves and their bodies, a lesson I continue to learn.

And really, my body has taken care of me all along. As I cried and wrote sad poems about my absent bio-dad, as I failed Italian class, as I explored my gift of teaching, and as I grappled through how to be a whole person when I felt so broken. Throughout it all, my lungs breathed, my blood pumped, my heart expanded as I experienced art, and my mind relished the challenges and avoided the things that felt unsafe. It supported me even when I didn't trust it. It sent me signals—it tried to communicate— throughout the turmoil. It did what bodies were built to do. It kept me alive. And as I healed, my body continued to support me and give me strength as I remembered how to trust—other people and, more importantly, myself.

Francis Bacon, *Self-Portrait*, 1956. Oil on canvas. Unframed: 78 x 54 in. (198.12 x 137.16 cm) Framed: 86 ⅛ x 62 ¼ x 3 ⅛ in. (218.76 x 158.12 x 7.94 cm). Collection of the Modern Art Museum of Fort Worth, Gift of The Burnett Foundation in Honor of Marla Price © The Estate of Francis Bacon. All rights reserved. / DACS, London / ARS, NY 2023. CR Number - 56-01

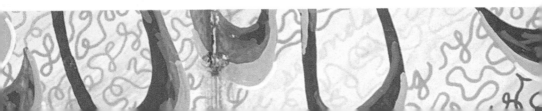

Self-Portrait

Striving to stay whole,
chaos threatens my senses.
How do I stay safe?

The arrival of my first daughter, Lily, shook up my life. Not only did she teach me the power and trustworthiness of my body, but her birth was also a catalyst for me to look with new eyes at the life she was born into. I was twenty-eight when she was born, and up until then, it was just me and my husband in a quiet, solitary life together. This steady, predictable life was precisely what I needed in those years as I slowly grew the capacity to heal and come to terms with my past and mental health. A small and consistent life with a stable and reliable spouse was best for me as I worked through many of my issues. Before I had Lily, I lived in a body, mind, and spirit at war with itself. Ultimately, I knew I was different; I was ashamed of who I was and didn't believe I was lovable. I had felt a brokenness that reverberated throughout my life, especially my physical body.

It wasn't until years of untangling and battling with the size of my body—showing distrust by not listening to its hunger cues, alternatingly starving it and overfeeding it, participating in our culture's obsession with controlling women through controlling their bodies—did I start to realize that something lived underneath all of that fighting. Not only did the suppression of my feelings lead to physical and emotional discomfort (chronic migraines, itching, and anxiety), but also a nervous system that was constantly sending my body into regular fight, flight, or freeze responses.

In my quest to always appear normal, have it together, and be perfect, I attempted to force myself into a box of what I perceived as an acceptable way for a body to be, both in size and in how it reacts to the world around it. When social stimulation, cacophonous sounds, distracting smells, or chaotic movement overwhelmed me, I pushed those things to the side to appear "normal." I didn't know what was happening, so I judged my reactions to these sensory stimuli. I escaped, hid, and did everything in my power to dull these feelings of sensory overwhelm through food or alcohol just to make it through. I learned to push myself far beyond my physical limits so that others wouldn't judge me. These situations upset my nervous system so much that I would come home exhausted after being overstimulated and overwhelmed. I recognize this feeling in *Self-Portrait* (1956) by Francis Bacon.

Distorted
Trapped in
the chaos of my mind
while my body drifts
Transparent
Untethered, agitated, uncomfortable
Floating, black, a void
Unanchored and searching
the buzzing static fighting to
overtake my presence
leaning forward willing
my body to stay
Stay normal
Stay small
Just to exist

Because of my social anxiety, sensory sensitivities, and shame about my size, my threat system was activated whenever I was outside my house and interacting with the world. It took a lot of time to replenish and repair once I was home because I didn't realize that I was having a nervous system response or how to navigate those physical and emotional sensations; I did the only things that I knew would help: video games and food. Video games allowed me to distract my mind and help me move my attention away from how terrible I felt. Food grounded me in my body, allowing me to feel something when my body was buzzing and going transparent from the overstimulation. The weight that I put on added a weighted blanket to protect me from my outside environment.

Even though it felt as if my nervous system was under attack, I didn't even recognize or register that I had these sensory sensitivities, partly because of my disconnect and war with my body, but partly because until I had children, I had never even heard of sensory processing disorder before. And then this baby arrived. She looked so much like me, and she still does. Her thick eyebrows above hooded, brown eyes, slightly upturned bulbous nose, dimpled chubby cheeks, exaggerated upper lip peak, and thick, unruly hair that can't decide if it's straight or wavy. When I looked at her, I saw my baby, this brand new person who didn't exist and now she did, but I also saw myself reflected back.

And she didn't just look like me but acted like me. I didn't know you could have an anxious baby that is a perfectionist, but somehow I had one, and I saw it in her. She wasn't quick to smile—too curious in her observations of the world and unsure about her role in it. At twelve months old, I knew she knew how to walk, but she just wasn't doing it. I knew she wouldn't do it until she knew she could do it right. As she grew, she was diagnosed with sensory processing disorder and later autism, and we invested in noise-canceling headphones and enrolled her in occupational therapy. And then eventually came a time when anxiety medication was needed for her. There was no shame or judgment about supporting her and her needs. She needed these things, so we provided them.

Until I could look at myself the same way, with neutrality and without shame, did I see that maybe something similar was happening to me. Perhaps I am not broken. Perhaps this is just how I am and how I have always been. Perhaps how my body reacts to sensory stimulation is not how other people's bodies react; maybe nothing is wrong with that. Just different. No trauma made my daughter sensitive to sounds, overwhelmed by people's energies, and scared of failure. No trauma incited her anxiety and hesitancies. She just was born that way. And maybe I was just born that way too. Perhaps I wasn't broken, needing to be fixed, but whole and needing acceptance and accommodations.

Looking at my sweet and sensitive baby, I couldn't imagine a world where she was unlovable. I looked at her little chubby cheeks, squishy thighs, and warm, vital body and couldn't imagine a world where every cell in that body was not perfect—no matter what size it was, no matter how it looked, and no matter its sensitivities or anxieties. She didn't have to earn her lovability. She just was. She deserved to love and be loved because she was a person on this earth. She arrived whole. It was hard to deny, looking into her eyes, filled with love, that I was not lovable too. Because not only did this little baby look up at me with love, but I was my mother's baby once, and I know she looked at me like this. And I know my mom loves me as powerfully as she ever did and loved me in the ways she could; she spent the first two weeks of Lily's life caring for us both.

So what happened then? How did that beautiful pure love I once had and accepted as truth get so distorted nearly beyond recognition? How could I so easily see myself in the *Self-Portrait* by Francis Bacon?

I looked at Lily and had this intense desire to prevent her from dealing with the low self-worth and shame that I was feeling. How do I prevent her from becoming what I had become? How do I make sure she never forgets she is loved? I realized that it can't be just words. I realized I needed to show her what it is like to own your own worth. I needed to heal so that she could see a model of what it looks like when someone honors who they are, who doesn't judge and shame herself for her natural way of being. Lily knowing she is lovable relied on me changing. Me healing. Me becoming. Me choosing wholeness every day. I had been on this healing journey for years but had reached a tipping point. It was no longer about me anymore. It was about her, too.

I look at that time with my first baby as a precious cocoon. The world stopped. No multiple jobs to distract me, no striving for the next thing, no time to consider what is next. Just time to admire and keep alive this new little being. I had entered motherhood as a battered caterpillar, full of all the toxic things I'd eaten up, and now it was time to change. It was time to truly disassemble who I was and put myself back together so that I could be (for myself and my daughter) who I have always known I could be. It started with a decision. A decision that I am likable and that I am lovable. Whether inside I truly believed it or not was irrelevant.

> **66** I pretended to be somebody
> I wanted to be until finally I became
> that person. Or he became me. **99**
> — Cary Grant

A cocoon implies that there is a before and an after. I inherently knew at this point that the before was done. The hardest part was over. The pain and anxiety were still real (the *Self-Portrait* was hanging in the shadows), but I had hope, motivation, and readiness for change. A caterpillar must become goo before she can become a majestic moth.

What amazes me about a cocoon, the space between a caterpillar and a moth, is that it's not a space of rest but a space of work. Inside the cocoon, the caterpillar transforms into an entirely different creature by digesting most of its own body and turning it into cells that form together to create the new insect. The caterpillar breaks down nearly everything it once was and becomes something new. But what's cool is that inside the caterpillar's body, small structures of the moth or butterfly are there from birth. Its true self is buried inside and must be strengthened and revealed. The beautiful moth was there all along, waiting inside the caterpillar.

I see this cocoon state before the transformation in *Self-Portrait* by Francis Bacon. He is in the goo, the bug soup. He is intangible, uncertain, and insecure. He crosses his legs and leans into them to hold himself together. He is coming apart and has reached a point where the pain of staying the same is greater than the pain of the transformation.

This transformational metaphor carried me and held me as a new mother. I knew, as all women do after their firstborn, that life would never be the same and that I would be changed hereafter. I had a new relationship with my body and a new person who would be watching and learning from me, and scraping by with anxiety and low self-worth no longer felt like a good enough life to lead. I always knew that the life I truly wanted was so much more expansive than the small life I had been living. I bargained that it was okay for me until then, but I couldn't let that happen to my little baby. She deserved more. And because of that, I then knew that I deserved more.

❊ ❊ ❊

I knew what I wanted—I wanted to feel free and whole. I wanted to feel the deep love for myself that I felt for my daughter. I wanted it for myself, but I wanted my daughter to be raised by someone who loved herself. So now it was time to do the work of change. Sometimes it is easier to be in pain and do nothing about it. Growth is painful. Change is uncomfortable. I'd avoided the pain and discomfort of change for many years, but I'd also avoided the growth and joy on the other side.

I knew that I had more authority than I had given myself permission to wield in my own life. I didn't know how to use this knowledge and power yet, but I could feel the change stirring—solid in my body—and that was enough.

Niki de Saint Phalle, *The Three Graces*, 1999.
© 2023 Niki Charitable Art Foundation / ARS, NY / ADAGP, Paris .
Photo by Elvert Barnes (CC BY-SA 2.0)

The Three Graces

Unburdened, they flow—
Light, unbound, giving no fucks.
I long to feel free.

When I think about the term wholeness, it feels full and embodied—the opposite of what we aim to accomplish by controlling and restricting our bodies. As women in society, we've learned that our fullness and wholeness are wrong, that we need to remove parts of our wholeness to be acceptable, and that life will only begin once we take up less space. Burdened under the weight of my anxiety, shame, and body dysmorphia, I longed for the freedom expressed in the *Nana* sculptures, particularly *The Three Graces*, of Niki de Saint Phalle.

As a woman, I know these artworks exist to celebrate me, my body, and the powerful, majestic bodies of all types of women worldwide. The sculptures from this series exude body positivity and energy. The women dance and soar through the air. Even when they sit, they look comfortable with patchwork patterns calling to mind a snuggle moment with a cozy quilt. These abstract and boldly-patterned women look fully alive and unencumbered.

It is revolutionary for a woman to be fully embodied—vital and bold. To exist fully in her own skin for herself at whatever size she is. When I look at these sculptures, I don't see women existing to be seen, consumed, or judged; I see women existing to live loud and free—wholly their own and of this world. I see women who don't care what others think of them, who don't waste their time and energy getting caught up in worry or toxic thoughts. They didn't change themselves to fit someone else's definition of who they should be.

They dance because it feels good to dance. They wear bold colors because they find color beautiful and pleasing to their eyes. They rest when they need to rest and play when they want to play. They know that their lives aren't perfect and that difficult emotions and situations will arise, but they have the self-trust, self-knowing, and resourcefulness to make it through anything. They love themselves and accept themselves no matter what they're feeling.

This is wholeness. It is a state of peace with yourself, of knowing you are not broken, of understanding and accepting all of the parts of you as they are now. Through the eyes of the *Nanas*, I see what is possible for me in my own life—to feel at ease, to release my heavy burdens, to set myself free.

❋ ❋ ❋

During that time after Lily's birth, I looked at my life intently and curiously. When I looked at this new baby, I wanted her to feel the love of the people surrounding her. And I wanted her examples to look like the *Nanas*. I didn't want her to be filled with anxiety like me; intuitively, I knew that whatever energy I was bringing underneath the surface of my actions, even if I couldn't put words to it at the time, would rub off on her. I wanted her to see what I have always known buried deep inside: I am powerful and worthy of love, care, and attention. I wanted her to have someone to look up to. A mom and a dad who loved her unconditionally—of course—but I wanted her to see me for who I knew I could be. So, I had to start not only healing from my past but creating the life that I needed and wanted in my present and future.

I thought about my own childhood and the things that worked for me. I liked how after second grade, when my mom married my dad, we lived in the same house until I moved away to college. I stayed in the same schools in the same feeder pattern and grew up with the same people.

(My struggles with social anxiety came in college and early adulthood after moving away from that built-in support system.) I was always a shy kid, for sure, but I did find my people. I wanted the same for my own kids. I also looked at my family—we had big family Christmases and events with siblings, nieces, nephews, cousins, uncles, aunts, and grandparents. We also had our church community. I was raised Catholic, and from the second grade on, we attended church every Sunday until I moved away. I was active in the youth group and had great fun there. My mom also worked from home as a daycare provider, so I always had her presence no matter what.

All those things provided community, friends, and family—none of which were a part of our life when I had Lily in 2009. Our families lived hours away, and although I had a few friends, all first-time moms understand that friendships change when you have kids. And these friendships were riddled with the remnants of my years of anxiety. They were built on a rocky foundation of my low self-esteem, and without a strong foundation of knowing I was loveable, they didn't have a chance to fully take root and grow.

Not only did I not have a stable community, but I also had a deep fear and discomfort around people. Having a first baby is lonely even when you have strong friendships, but it is even more challenging when no one you know has children. Suddenly, it was a new world both bigger and smaller than it once was, with new priorities, new things to think about, and new experiences to process. After a few months, I realized I had a deep need for connection and community. I wanted to believe that I was not alone. I wanted to believe that having close and connected friends was possible. I wanted to believe that life could be greater than what mine had become. To do this, I knew I had to expand. I knew I would have to take some risks. I was willing to create an environment for myself that enabled deep healing, but it was going to be a lot of work.

✳ ✳ ✳

I knew I needed real love and connection to heal my deep wounds of disconnection. So I set out to make some friends—some other new moms who I could connect with and who had children my daughter could play with. What I ultimately decided I wanted was a church community but without religion. I wanted family friends. I wanted people who I could count on for support, people who would watch my kids in an emergency, people I could cry to if I was going through something, all those things. I wanted to have my people around me—just like the *Nanas*—all of us strong, solid, and supportive of each other. I knew a church could provide the structure to help me through the anxiety of meeting new people. It would give me events and a welcoming environment that doesn't make people question why you are there.

But I had a problem. I identified as an atheist at the time. Where do you find a church when you are an atheist? So I started googling and found a Humanist family group on meetup.com called the Dallas Brights, now defunct. The group had family get-togethers, but it also had playdates during the week. So my husband and I showed up nervously to our first family event with the Dallas Brights at a park with our eight-month-old, who couldn't even walk let alone play at a park. There I met Melissa with a baby about the same age as mine, who was also an atheist, also a teacher, also in the arts. I enjoyed our conversation and chatted with a few others, but Melissa stood out. Like I used to feel about my sister, I was pretty sure that Melissa was way too cool for me. This time, though, I suspended my fear. I decided I was "cool enough" for Melissa (even though cool enough isn't even a thing as an adult). I saw in her the possibility of the freedom of the community bond in the *Nanas*, and I jumped.

I began attending regular playdate meetups with the group, and as I started to engage with some of the other moms, I inherently knew that these were my people. They were interesting, liberal, and atheist. They were my people, I knew they were, but I still didn't have the confidence to truly see how I fit. I could see that they were my people, but I didn't trust that they knew I was their people. I loved the conversations (having a baby gave me something easy to talk about), but these early playdates required a lot of strength and courage. I would leave filled with so much anxiety—second guessing everything I said or did, worried that they didn't like me, and afraid that they wished I wasn't there and they were just tolerating my presence.

But something in me decided I wouldn't allow that anxious voice to determine my actions. I invited families for dinner to get to know them better, and I was shocked when they said yes. I actively took chances and risks and dealt with the anxious fallout afterward. I also decided that instead of repeatedly telling myself that they didn't want me there and interpreting all of their actions through a negative lens, I would start looking for evidence to the contrary. I tried seeing things through the jubilance and confidence of those *Nanas*. I began to look for evidence that they wanted me around.

And guess what happens when you start to look for something? Often, you start to find it. I would receive a note from someone who was just thinking of me. Or someone would say something that made me feel seen and heard for who I am. Or I'd get a compliment. Or I'd watch and see who would voluntarily sit next to me. Etc. I've always watched things like that keenly, but it's always been to look for proof that I was not wanted or was different. I would actively look for judgment against me. As I allowed myself to flip my perspective, I was starting to see proof that I belonged in this group.

After a year of attending these playdates regularly, Melissa and I discussed how fun it would be to trick or treat at Halloween together. Yes! Something I always wanted—friends that were more like family. And we talked about whether we make it a big group event with all of the Brights or invite a few people. She then said to me something I will never forget. She said, "This is a holiday; this is my family. I want people around who I really love and want to be with. Friends worthy of spending my and my child's holiday with." It gives me chills even today to write that because it made such an impact on me. Here she was saying, "Cindy. I want you in my life. I love you, and you are important to me." I honestly couldn't believe it; it remains a pivotal moment in my journey. I chose to believe and trust her, just as I was learning to trust myself.

This friend group eventually broke off on our own, but what became clear to me was that for the first time in my adult life, I was learning how to exist in a social structure. This group was a cocoon for my self-confidence. I went into this group broken but hopeful, and these beautiful friends provided the container for the growth of my self-worth. They surround me with their fullness just as I see the *Nanas*. We became connected and bonded through our shared experiences. In our circle, I was learning to trust, and they supported me through it. Each time I saw them, it became a choice to believe that I belonged in that room, and that was not an easy thing to accept in the beginning. In the early days of our friendship, when our babies were little, we would have these weekly epic eight-hour-long playdates. The kids would run amok, and the moms would chat, eat, and play games our way through breakfast, lunch, and nearly dinner at someone's house before we had to pull ourselves away to avoid traffic and get home so the littles could sleep. We'd get home and immediately start chatting again online, often with babies attached to our boobs or sitting on the floor in a dark room to comfort an overtired or scared toddler. We really couldn't get enough of each other. I loved these times getting to know each other, and it felt so good to be seen as who I am, just as I was.

✳ ✳ ✳

Those playdates are some of my fondest memories. Still, I remember how those long days wrecked me—having just spent the whole day dismissing anxiety and dealing with my sensory sensitivities. As I drove away, I always beelined to the closest McDonalds or Starbucks because food, Coke, and iced coffee were the only things I knew that would help ease my nervous system just a little bit. I spent every evening after these playdates in bed, not only in over-stimulated mode from the parade of kazoos, the screaming kids, the Super Simple Songs YouTube channel playing loudly from the other room, and the clingy babies, but exhausted from all of the social interaction, replaying things I said or didn't say, analyzing what was said to me or not said to me.

While these experiences were difficult, I knew I needed them. I knew they were instrumental to my healing and ability to love myself and break free from the armor I had built over all parts of me. I felt as if I was simultaneously breaking myself down while also burgeoning into the fullness of myself, becoming more the person I was meant to be week by week, month by month, year by year. So even though it took a few days to recover, I forced myself to go. With each interaction, I was building new muscles, breaking up some of the muscle fibers so that they could grow stronger with each new connection.

My friends surrounded me in my recovery in spirit through our group chat. I could be honest with them about how I was feeling, and in turn, they were honest with me. I learned that my presence was important and loved, but I also discovered that they had some of the same insecurities that I have. They also questioned their value in the room, second-guessed and regretted things they said or did, and were overwhelmed and exhausted but energized by our relationship. They taught me so much about myself by being my witness and mirror. I was starting to realize that perhaps these fears and questions I would ask about my place in the group were more universal than I had believed. This was revolutionary for me to see. I've always felt like an alien, and finally I found some other aliens like me.

When I look at Niki de Saint Phalle's The Three Graces, I see these three women at such peace and joy together. I felt unsafe showing any emotion, including positive ones. Joy was not a state that ever felt solid in my body, and I often shut down glimpses of joy as quickly as they arrived. My new friends taught me to not only allow joy but to relish in it. To spin and twirl and celebrate it. To be boisterous and alive. As our kids aged out of their playdate era, our times together morphed into nights and weekends—spending hours playing games, drinking, telling stories, and cracking jokes. I allowed them to see all of my parts—my rough edges, quiet humor, overwhelming curiosity, competitiveness, and love of Salt n' Pepa and TLC.

Although people fell off from the group, moved away, or left over the years (we all were broken in our own ways, with our own anxieties and traumas), it started with fun and kids. Later it changed and evolved as we grew in our friendship, and I can honestly say I was having more fun in my thirties than in my twenties. Those friendships developed into deep love and understanding, being there for each other through divorces, life changes, family drama, and pandemics. I am so grateful for those conversations that started with small talk about our babies to discovering I had found my chosen family.

> **"** Sometimes, he thought to himself in a house in a cerulean sea, you were able to choose the life you wanted. And if you were of the lucky sort, sometimes that life chose you back. **"**
> — T.J. Klune in The House in the Cerulean Sea

I imagine us like *The Three Graces* dancing together, each sculpted woman facing in a different direction yet remaining one unit. We each started out alone and broken in our own ways, and through our relationship, we found ourselves as individuals and as a group. We are now stronger as individuals and stronger together as we continue to deepen our relationship, learn to better communicate what we want and need, and learn how to stretch to the edges of our friendship. More than thirteen years into our friendship, these women are the backdrop for the rest of my story—witnessing me and surrounding me as I heal, as I learn who I am and how to love myself as I am, how to discover my magic, and how to harness it.

Madalyn, Paige, and Amber, I love you forever.

Even though I knew the importance of these times, I wasn't in tune enough with my mind, body, and spirit to navigate through this recovery without some repercussions. It feels counter-culture to say that during one of the happiest times of my life, when my babies were still babies and when I met my beautiful friends who became family, was also the time when I gained the most weight. I gained over one hundred pounds in those five years, from 2009 to 2014. But I don't look at that one hundred pounds with shame or disgust, as many women do with their "before pictures." I look at that one hundred pounds with love and gratitude. In those cocoons of blankets, pillows, video games, iced coffee, and french fries, after overloading my senses with social interaction and stimulation, I healed my relationship with myself.

I learned that I am lovable.
I learned that I have value at any size and without trying to be perfect.

I noticed and labeled my sensory sensitivities for the first time ever.

I learned how to work with them rather than push them down.

I learned that anxiety is treatable with medication and that I don't have to constantly tolerate feeling bad as a punishment to myself.

I learned I am worthy of feeling good.

I learned I can let loose the reins of control, perfectionism, and insecurities for a minute and not lose everyone I love. In fact, I learned the opposite. When I let go of control, I get closer to people rather than scare them away. Releasing control allows me to be more present and available for connection to others and myself.

I learned how to laugh freely. I learned how to have fun.

I learned I can embody one of Niki de Saint Phalle's *Nanas*—bold, vital, and free.

As I learned those lessons, I built up the capacity and the support to go after the big dreams that had always tickled the back of my mind. If I had to do it all over, I'd choose to gain that weight again and again because that weight gave me the comfort and support I needed at the time to make significant changes in my life, including starting my business and traveling more. And those changes made it possible for me to have the life I have now, the relationships I have now, the business I have now, and the understanding and vitality I have now.

I'd lived most of my life not feeling safe in my body, and that weight provided me with the safety I needed to participate in activities that felt profoundly unsafe. You can't create when your threat system is activated; the only thing you can do when your threat system is activated is survive. The safety I learned to feel in my body gave me the space to create the life I wanted to live.

Only when my nervous system had calmed down and gotten me out of that constant threat response was I able to see my body as a partner in my life, not as a barrier. My body cared for me through all the sadness and anxiety. It was doing its best to keep me safe by sending me signals. When I started to remove the shame and the judgment and started to think about what I wanted in my life and how my body already supported me, I began to recognize the wisdom that my body contains.

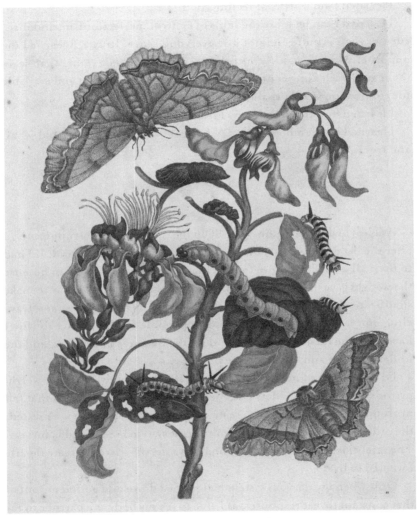

Maria Sibylla Merian, *Caterpillars, Butterflies and Flower*, 1705.
15 x 11 ⅛ in. (38.1 x 28.26 cm) Hand-colored etching and engraving.
Minneapolis Institute of Art, The Minnich Collection The Ethel Morrison Van DerLip Fund, 1966

Caterpillars, Butterflies, and Flower

Safe, cocooned, she waits
for her body to reveal.
Its answer: emerge.

How does the moth feel when ready to break out of its cocoon?
How does it know it is ready?
How does it build strength to make that first move?
How does it leave behind who it once was to embody the becoming?
How does it take the first step into a new life?

Erik Johansson, *Grow with Progress*, 2021. Image courtesy of the artist

Grow with Progress

A choice, the first step.
Strength, wisdom, found on the path—
A step toward me.

Until the point in my adult life when I had my babies and met my friends, I didn't see a way out of my pain. I felt resigned to living a small life, even though there was always a part of me wanting something bigger and better. The staircase of what it would take to get out of that small life felt insurmountable. But, things for me were shifting.

In Erik Johansson's surreal photograph, *Grow with Progress*, a woman stands at the bottom of a cement staircase that cuts through rocks by the ocean, with green plants spottily poking through the rocky crevices. The woman is taking a step forward—her gaze set at the top of the stairs. As the stairs progress higher, the scale and perspective change. The stairs get bigger and bigger until, at the top, the woman's calves and feet are shown again in the picture, maybe ten times larger than she is at the bottom. The sky is blue, sunny, and partly cloudy, and only a tiny sliver of the ocean peeks through the rocks.

When I look at the photograph, I imagine the perspectives of the two women. The world is small for the woman at the bottom of the stairs. She only can see big rocks around her and a daunting staircase ahead. She is the moth, cramped in its cocoon, not yet knowing if it has the strength to break free, to become what she is meant to be. The photograph (and its title) seem to suggest that with every step forward, she will grow a little bit to climb each step more easily as they also increase in size incrementally. The top step is more than half the size of the woman at the bottom. If she stays the same size while climbing, she may not ever get up that final step, but I as the viewer assume that with action, moving forward toward her goal, she will grow to meet the next challenge.

In the early days of my motherhood, when my two girls were small and my soul friendships were new, my confidence and self-worth had grown. I felt big enough and strong enough to tackle that first step forward like the woman in the photograph. My life had a new purpose, and I finally had a handle on my mental health. I could genuinely call myself happy. It was like coming out of a decade-long fog. Once that fog lifted, I was able to take a look around me and really see my life with new eyes.

During the next phase of my life, I made a series of choices that may have appeared sudden from an outsider's point of view. Just as you might come upon a butterfly instantly fluttering away from its chrysalis as if it never was a caterpillar, there came a moment when I knew it was time to move, to fly. There was no more time to waste. I was ready to leave the casings of my old life behind, just like the butterfly. And that moment came in the form of a podcast I listened to as I spent my days caring for my babies. It sent a jolt through my life that forever changed its course.

This podcast episode focused on an entrepreneur traveling the world with her family, and in the moments after that episode wrapped, I realized that I wanted nothing more than to do that. My parents are travelers, and I caught the travel bug as a child. My love of travel might seem paradoxical when held in the same hand as my social anxiety and sensory sensitivities, but travel comforts me. Maybe it's partly because my parents introduced me to the wonders of traveling, but I also know that my comfort stems from my anonymity when I venture into a new environment. This anonymity of not knowing anyone and no one knowing me gives me solace and allows my anxiety and constant self-consciousness to melt a little.

In these new places, I release the expectation to impress and the anxiety and fear around being judged because I will most likely never see this cast of characters again. I also love the energy and excitement of a new place—delighting in unexplored foods, art, culture, sights, and customs.

New places are portals of possibilities and dreams of alternate lives where we can be anything we want. Travel is a way to exist in a state of delight and wonder, and as a not-yet-aware ADHDer, I lived for delight and wonder. In high school, my English and Humanities teacher took groups of students to Europe every summer, and I went, sacking a lot of groceries to pay for much of that trip. I did a summer study abroad trip to Italy in college (still paying for that, thanks to student loans). And in high school, I was informally voted by my friends as "Most Likely to Move to Europe." I've got a trophy and everything.

But that travel bug had been dormant for so long because we didn't have the funds to travel with my husband in college and me working in low-paying education and non-profit jobs. That podcast episode was the spark that lit the kindling that I had been quietly collecting for a long time. Or maybe a sound from the outside beckoned the moth to break free. The outcome is the same whether we use the moth metaphor or the power of fire. Something changed in me, and I was ready, just like the woman in Johannson's photograph. She is already planning her next step. She knows the ocean is near. She can probably hear the waves, smell the salt water, and feel the thick humid air and even perhaps the mist of the waves as it drifts over the rocks. Its siren song calls to her, and she steps forward to greet it.

At first, I imagine her surrounded by rocks with the staircase hidden or at her back, but she knows she needs to see the ocean. She longs to gaze at the horizon. She yearns for the space, freedom, and relief of that moment when her eye meets the vast expanse of the world. The lively green plants poke through the rocks giving her hope that there is new life beyond her rocky cage. In the moments after finishing that podcast episode, I took an inventory of my life and decided to change it. At that moment, I recognized I was physically and financially stuck. I realized I wasn't living the life I wanted, the one I had always dreamed about. I was merely living the safety and consistency of a regular American life. Married. Two kids. Homeownership (it was a money pit, but hey, we owned it). Middle-class jobs. Paycheck to paycheck. I was merely surviving and moving from circumstance to circumstance, following the next expected steps. I'm not judging this at all. After living in chaotic internal anguish for so long, I fought hard for this ordinary, stable life.

> 66 Sometimes I can hear my bones straining under the weight of all the lives I'm not living. 99
> — Jonathan Safran Foer in *Extremely Loud and Incredibly Close*

I felt like I was living someone else's life, though. I didn't even know who I was anymore. Deep down, I'd always known that a different person was waiting to be let out—not one of those cliche thin people hiding in the fat person, but someone full of life and vitality. She was in there somewhere, and I finally saw glimpses of her in my new friendships. With my perfectionism, shame, body image issues, and wanting to fit in, I had been stuffing down the true desires I had for my life and building a nice thick suit of armor to keep all of my hopes and dreams locked in tight. I felt stuck in this hamster wheel, but I knew that the wheel was not leading anywhere, and furthermore, beneath all this armor, I was not even a hamster.

So I made the choice to step off. (Actually, I flew off the hamster wheel. Turns out, I am a majestic bird, or maybe I am one of Maria Sibylla Merian's moths.) I took an inventory of my life. Getting unstuck involves a whole lot of things, but at the beginning, it consists of knowing three essential things—knowing where you want to go (or more accurately, how you want to feel when you get there), what is keeping you from getting there, and knowing that you have agency—that you have the power and the ability to get yourself out of this feeling of stuckness.

I clearly saw what I wanted—freedom, adventure, experience, joy. And, since I no longer felt the crushing weight of my mental illness and joy was at hand in my new friendships, I clearly saw several of the main issues holding me back—keeping me from being truly free. The most significant problems I saw then were my crippling debt (credit cards and student loans), low income, and minimal time off that would support the freedom I wanted. Also, my physical body limited my stamina and energy. But for the first time, I knew that I could make this happen. Bolstered by the confidence of the changes I had made in the last few years, the hard work I had done to feel better, and the self-trust that I had started to build in myself, I saw that I was finally capable of achieving the life I wanted. Suddenly the staircase, the path out, began to form. I immediately made a series of choices that set me on that path to freedom. Like the woman in the photograph, I took my first step toward where I wanted to go, how I wanted to feel, and who I wanted to be.

> **❝ As you start to walk on the way, the way appears. ❞**
>
> — Rumi

✳ ✳ ✳

The woman from the podcast episode was a blogger, and I, having started 6,000 blogs over the last ten years but always fizzling out after a few months, was amazed that she was able to completely support her family on this year-long trip around the world just by writing on the internet. At this point in my career, I was teaching art and knew my way of teaching and connecting with art was special. How I look at art is something we're not necessarily trained in in art education classes. The internet was empty of resources for art appreciation and art history unless you wanted to copy a famous artist or give a boring lecture, so starting a blog writing about works of art and how to teach them was a natural and easy choice. There was a need in the market-place at the same time as there was a need in my life for a take-charge purpose.

However, starting a business didn't come out of nowhere. Honestly, I've always been an entrepreneur. I just hadn't had a business idea that stuck—from creating and selling hand-drawn presidential campaign posters door to door as a kid to selling block print greeting cards to writing a business plan for an art cafe, I always knew I had the entrepre-neurial spirit. But that drive was stifled by anxiety, fear, avoidance, and living from circumstance. I had spent my life feeling like a square peg in a round hole, stuffing down the ever-present itch for greatness, but with that one choice after listening to that podcast episode, it all changed.

I leaned into the fear and dreams, and I got to work. I wrote my first blog post and designed my website that same day. It started as Two Muses Homeschool, then The Art Curator for Kids, and eventually landed as Art Class Curator.

Art Class Curator wasn't a big success right away; I had a lot to learn about finding an audience and marketing, selling, and delivering my education products. I had to put in a lot of hours of creating content, sending emails, creating social media posts, answering customer emails, and more—all while working full-time and caring for two little girls. I spent a lot of time and money to create success. It was a few years before I was at a point where the business replaced my meager online teaching salary. Still, there was a switch that had been flipped, an ignited spark, and a forward momentum that was incredibly energizing to me. I knew on some cellular level that this business was the right thing for me to do. I knew that if I kept doing it, it would work. I don't know how I knew. I had complete faith in the process and trust in my ability to make it happen.

And I started to see how my work was spreading the magic of art beyond my own classrooms and galleries. Teachers worldwide used my innovative artwork lessons and ideas from my membership site, Curated Connections, to influence the next generation. It was thrilling. Anytime I truly stepped back and allowed myself to fathom the number of kids impacted by my work, I would be overwhelmed to tears. Profound. And I loved the energy and excitement of building something new, helping people, and fully stepping into and owning my expertise and gifts for the first time in my life.

It was like I was being pulled up the stairs from Johannson's photograph by an unseen force. The ocean breeze swept me up, and my faith, excitement, and hyper-focus kept me along the straight and narrow path. It wasn't until I got midway up the staircase that it started to get really hard. With success comes the need for consistency, systems, order, delegation, and managing a team. I struggled as I climbed those increasingly steep steps as the work morphed out of the exciting start-up energy and into maintenance and growth energy. The title of this artwork is Grow with Progress, and I did absolutely grow with my own progress. Running a business and putting your creative work out into the world is more vulnerable and intense than I expected when I started. It opens you up to criticism, forces you to face all your insecurities, and puts you in a near-constant state of uncertainty. I grew in leaps and bounds, but you don't know what you don't know when you start out, so that growth I found wasn't necessarily in alignment with that straight path through the rocks.

When I started, my original goal was to be able to pay off my debt and replace my and my husband's salaries by the time my youngest daughter turned ten so we could travel around the world. I could easily see that straight path to the ocean, one step at a time. But a few years in, I realized that growth is not a linear, upward path.

✳ ✳ ✳

This artwork, I'm learning, is a lie. It's overly simplified and doesn't reflect the nuance of how life actually is, or maybe more like, how life should be. We are led to believe by so many in the personal development industry, by diet culture, by the American dream, by puritanical work ethic, that one can just work hard all the way up to the top—follow this four-point system and success is yours. But that's not how it works at all. There is no top. There is no one singular arrival.

> **"** She had thought...that she would never fail again. She had thought she arrived. But life was always arriving. There was always another gate to pass through. (Until, of course, there wasn't.) **"**
>
> — Gabrielle Zevin in *Tomorrow, and Tomorrow, and Tomorrow*

Growth is an up-and-down roller coaster. It's an M.C. Escher trippy illustration or the stairs changing at Hogwarts. What happens when shit hits the fan? When a hail storm wrecks every house in your town or when a novel coronavirus overtakes the whole globe? What happens when you have a big success followed by an even bigger disappointment or when your anxiety overtakes your system for an entire year and you burn out every aspect of your nervous system and have to rebuild your life and work from scratch?

Or what happens when you change your mind? When the last six years are spent climbing that one straight staircase to the sea, then you realize you maybe should have climbed the rocks instead. Or maybe you don't want to go to the ocean anymore, and the forest is where you want to be? Or perhaps your whole goal is to take your family on a trip around the world and then find out (many years after the plan is in motion) that everyone but you in your family is autistic and three-fourths have anxiety, and traveling around the world with no home base would be their worst nightmares. What happens when your dream life is the direct opposite of theirs?

Where in this artwork is the permission to change your mind?

Permission to falter?

Permission to slow down, rest in a soft and comfortable place, and regroup?

Permission to do something outside the laid out, expected path—outside the steps?

Life is softer and gentler than this artwork's cold hard rocks make it out to be. And I have been too hard on myself for most of my life (and honestly, even now, though I am much better). I was nothing but hard edges masking my raw, sensitive self inside.

I pushed, and I pushed, and I pushed.

I pushed to be the smartest.

I pushed to be the most perfect.

I pushed to be the most accomplished.

And that didn't stop when I started my business. That inner voice that bemoaned my sales if they didn't reach an arbitrary goal, sent my nervous system into disarray at the slightest criticism from a customer, and censored out any drop of vulnerability or imperfection from every piece of communication, email, or social media post. That same inner critic questioned my parenting, how I ate, how I moved through the world, and how I spoke to people.

I had to make a lot happen to get to the point where I could start and run this business and make these changes in my life. I did a lot of work on my self-worth, my confidence, my body image, my relationships with others, and my relationship with myself. Taking that first step forward up the staircase of my ambitions set into motion the next phase on my path to becoming whole—moving my guiding questions away from why am I so broken and how can I make the pain stop to how do I want to be and how do I want to feel. Art led me to these answers. It enables me to step off the stairs and scrabble across uncharted territory on my own terms. Sometimes moving towards a precipice, but other times moving towards something more unexpected, life-giving, and soul-filling.

Roger Kastel, *Jaws*, 1975

Jaws

Right, left, right, left, right:
Keep swimming and you'll be safe.
Danger lurks beneath.

During the first fifteen years of my adult life, I thought if I powered through the pain and hid what was going on inside, I could eventually ambition my way through everything. Surely I would arrive at the place of "making it." When I finally arrived, the outside and inside would make sense together. Having the perfect job, the perfect location, the perfect belongings, the perfect friends, the perfect weight—all of it would equal the perfect me. I would be there and ready, waiting on the other end, at the top of the stairs in Erik Johansson's *Grow with Progress*.

I bargained that most of the solutions to my problems were external, and I could just push and push and push, and eventually, things would get better. And that strategy did work for a while; I pushed and pushed and pushed myself through the discomfort of socializing until I started to feel at ease and welcome. For most of my life, I worked two jobs simultaneously—working through school, then working full-time while teaching community college at night. I was used to the hustle, so when I started my business, it was natural to keep pushing to turn it into a success through sheer will and determination.

My pain and distracting myself from it was a driver, my passion for art was a driver, the joy and satisfaction I felt when teaching was a driver, and those things motivated me to keep going and going and going. My work as an art educator was one of the only places I truly felt valuable as a person, so it was easy to dive into that work because of the thrill and excitement it gave me, but also the peace and purpose. When I was working, I could be creative, I could forget about my struggles, and I could just allow my full brilliance to come out.

In the early days of my business, in addition to the job of taking care of two little girls, I worked a full-time job and grew the business by night and weekend. I worked around the clock, and my ADHD superpower of hyper-focus allowed me to do this and forget important wellness things like movement, eating regular meals, and going outside into the sun. I was the energizer bunny and kept pushing and pushing and pushing until success! And it came; my first big launch was in 2017, and after having busted my ass for three years, I finally was making enough money in the business to quit my full-time employment and focus solely on the business and my family.

I didn't use this opportunity to slow down, however. I kept pushing and moving forward—investing in business programs, attending conferences, listening to podcast after podcast, experimenting with all of the ideas I learned in those conferences and podcasts—working to 10x the success of my last launch. That's what all the internet online marketing gurus said I should do—gotta shoot for that seven-figure business. Nothing but forward momentum was tolerated. I was like a great white shark who had to keep swimming to breathe. They get oxygen as the water is pushed into their mouths through their gills. Without that forward momentum, they suffocate. I couldn't slow down because the discomfort would set in when I slowed down. The "negative" emotions I worked so hard to overcome would creep in. The anxiety would catch in my chest, making it hard to take a deep breath. So I kept working to keep the anxiety at a distance and the success close.

66 She understands what it means
to never be able to stop moving,
lest you find yourself unable to breathe. 99
— Shelby Van Pelt in *Remarkably Bright Creatures*

At some level, I understood that feeling any discomfort would stop me mid-stroke, so I did everything I could to push these emotions down through distraction and repression. I can see this now, but if you had asked me then, I would have told you that I was the happiest I have ever been during the early years of my business. And I was immensely happy. I had arrived at a great place—the top of the proverbial stairs. I was traveling again. I attended conferences nationwide, met interesting people, traveled to Europe multiple times, and even spent a week in Japan with my sister during cherry blossom season! I had a beautiful business making a real difference in the world. I had beautiful children, hilarious friends, and a devoted husband who loved me dearly. We finally had a stable income with enough money to meet our basic needs with a little room to play.

I was living that full vital life of my dreams, but an undercurrent of anxiety was simmering underneath my policy of "just keep swimming." Something was lurking beneath the surface that I was avoiding.

Here comes the shark.

The iconic artwork from the *Jaws* movie poster, an original painting by Roger Kastel, shows my undercurrent perfectly. In the painting, a nude woman, the great white's first victim in the movie, Chrissie Watkins, swims at the ocean's surface. Her eyes are closed; she is blissfully unaware of what lurks below. Under her, in the dense blue water, a giant great white shark, Bruce of course, swims up with his mouth open—full of gangly, sharp, chaotic, and absolutely terrifying teeth. His open mouth is as wide as Chrissie is tall. He's waiting to gulp her up in one decisive bite.

We know what's coming, but Chrissie doesn't. She isn't aware of the danger lurking; she can't see it through the darkness of the sea or hear it through her pounding heart and increased blood flow, the ocean waves crashing in the distance, and her freestyle strokes splashing by her ears. She probably feels free, happy, invigorated, and maybe even at peace—the water sliding past her nude skin, the endorphins rushing through her body, dopamine sending waves of pleasure, and adrenaline pumping through her bloodstream and creating excitement with the rebelliousness of her risqué actions. Her nervous system was doing all the right things to give her a satisfying, robust experience of her human vitality.

Starting a business based on my passion, skills, and drive and step ping out of the societal expectation of a nine to five was my version of skinny dipping. In the beginning, when my business was just me and my whims and energy, I could learn, experiment, and play. The creation process of the business—building the brand, doing the tech, making the products, writing the content. Each of those things probably released the same hormones that flooded through the soon-to-be-eaten swimmer. My ADHD brain craved feel-good brain chemicals, and my business provided that dopamine left and right—the cha-ching of a new sale, the satisfaction of solving a problem, a beautiful comment saying how my work impacted people. Sending an email to thousands of people or posting something personal on social media, especially with all of the social baggage from my past, felt scary and risky, so my body would flood with adrenaline at doing something so vulnerable. And for a while, I loved every minute of it.

I could see how suddenly my time was no longer tied to dollars. If I spent an hour teaching a community college class at the time, I would make thirty-two dollars—whether I showed a movie in class, did a lecture, or just let the students study for the next test. How hard I worked had no bearing on my pay at the end of the day. But now? I could spend an hour making something to sell, and then it could maybe sell ten, twenty, or one hundred times of that thirty-two dollars in the present and the years to come. I could see the future payoff with each task even if no dollars were coming in immediately. I had a crystal clear vision of where this business could take me, and I had 100 percent trust that if I just kept working, the results I wanted would come. Never before had I had such trust in anything, let alone myself.

But what would happen to Chrissie if she were to keep swimming and swimming and swimming. Okay, one, she will definitely get eaten by that shark, but I'll get to Bruce later. Physically, depending on her fitness level, she will start feeling the effects of that constant movement. Her muscles are going to begin to tire. She might start to get cramps, and her speed will decrease as the power in her muscles wears out. Her lung capacity will diminish, and her heart will reach its maximum capacity.

The adrenaline that's giving her that excited rush will also take a toll on her body. The other side of adrenaline is anxiety. Excitement and anxiety can feel exactly the same sometimes. Adrenaline (the hormone epinephrine) breaks down sugars in her liver to boost some quick energy. It's there to support her during stressful times—making her more focused and ready to respond to dangers, distracting her from any discomfort her body feels so that she can push through the pain to escape this dangerous situation. However, existing too long and often in this stress state can negatively affect her system. It can lead to heart damage, headaches, high blood pressure, an inability to sleep (which will then cause its own problems), and anxiety (WebMD, 2021).

So Dory's mantra of "Just Keep Swimming" from *Finding Nemo* may work for a fish built for constant swimming, but if Chrissie were to keep swimming forever, some bad things would start to happen even without Bruce waiting to gulp her up. And that's what started to happen to me. The continuous pushing started to have physical repercussions—causing all sorts of physical ailments and discomforts—bouts of anxiety and depression, heartburn, chronic migraine headaches, essential tremor, chronic itching, mysterious rashes, and dizziness. I was put on medicine after medicine to treat the symptoms, and then those medicines were masking some symptoms but causing others. Because I was keeping my mind so engaged and working around the clock, I couldn't sleep, so I had to take sleeping pills, which ended up causing more symptoms.

And that grab for the medicine bottles as a solution to every twinge in my body furthered those instincts that the answers to my problems were external. Once I finally started to slow my pace, I didn't know which way was up or how I could find the shore. I felt like I was doomed to live the rest of my life uncomfortable and in pain as test after test revealed no physiological cause. I tried allergy tests, elimination diets, and gut health protocols. I saw my primary care doctor, a neurologist, an allergist, a naturopathic doctor, an acupuncturist, a chiropractor, a reiki practitioner, and a hypnotist. Long story short—there was nothing actually wrong with me. Doctors didn't know the cause, so they just treated the symptoms. "It's just going to be something you have to live with," said my primary care doctor while I gave him my most infuriated look of disbelief. It's pretty safe to say that I was on a crash course to the big gulp from Bruce.

> **"** Lydia feels like a cracked egg, and she doesn't know if she's the shell or the yolk or the white. She is scrambled. **"**
> —Jeannine Cummins in *American Dirt*

It didn't stop with physical symptoms though. Some red flags started to pop up (you know, the ones they put on the beach to tell swimmers not to go into the water because it isn't safe there), and I ignored them. I haven't rewatched the movie (and I'm not gonna—too scary), but I'm wondering if there was a red flag at the beach the day Chrissie took her swim, warning her to stay out of the water. After having written blog posts and email newsletters every week and multiple times per week for several years, I started to be unable to write. I lost all confidence in myself as a writer and passed the writing on to someone on my team.

The lessons we released monthly for my membership for art teachers? I stopped being able to write those too. I hired a brilliant educator to write them. And then eventually, I stopped being able to even read them. I coined it as having trust in my team, delegating, etc., but I know I was really avoiding something big. There was a feeling in my body that was trying to give me a message about my work, and I was doing everything possible to ignore the feeling—that internal voice. Instead of listening to my inner wisdom, I began to rely on the voices of the course creators and online marketing gurus I followed. I no longer trusted my voice and used their scripts for email sequences, videos, and product launches. I put my creativity in a treasure chest and sent it to the bottom of the sea.

✳ ✳ ✳

And where was the art, you might be wondering? Oh yes, the ART. The one thing that has always guided me through my struggles and challenges? The thing that brought me to my truest self? The thing that connects me to passion and connection and love and energy? Yes. Where was the ART?

It was all around me, but I stopped looking at it.

Only when I traveled would I visit museums, and even then, I only allowed myself to look through the lens of how I would teach it, what lesson I would write about it, or how I would share about my visit on my business social media. My enthusiastic and energetic team would share artworks they found interesting in our dedicated inspiration Slack channel, and I wouldn't even click the links. Art, the most important thing that has been driving me my whole life, started becoming a source of anxiety. It started to become an afterthought. An annoyance even. I lost my personal connection to it—or maybe I was just ignoring it. Somewhere inside of me, I knew if I allowed art to touch my heart and guide me, it would tell me to stop or, at the very least, slow down. And there was no way I could allow that.

✳ ✳ ✳

Faintly in the background, I could hear it, though. The opening to the *Jaws* theme music by John Williams, *dun, dun-nuh, dun-nuh-dun, duh-nuh-dun-nuh, dun dun dun dun dun dun dun dun DUN DUN DUN DUN DUN DUN DUN DUN DUN DUN DUN DUN.* You can too, right?

The composition starts with just piano, then a drum, followed by blasts of horns, and then more instruments—strings and woodwinds—slowly coming in, increasing the tension, the danger, and the chaos.

> *dun*—me working way too many hours and ignoring my physical and emotional needs—*dun-nuh*—me overscheduling myself and not giving myself space to be and breathe—*dun-nuh-dun*—me listening to others telling me how to run my business instead of listening to my inner voice—*duh-nuh-dun-nuh*—me stopping writing—*dun dun dun dun dun dun dun dun*—me stopping looking at art—*DUN DUN DUN*—me pushing down the anxiety all of this brings up—*DUN DUN DUN*—me knowing something is wrong, but ignoring it—*DUN DUN DUN*—my skin is inflamed and itchy, and my head aches daily—*DUN DUN DUN.*

As I pushed and worked toward goals that the online business world told me I should have and leaned into my role as a "responsible business owner" instead of a "passionate creative," I fervently swam further and further from the shores of my own wellbeing, from the sands of my own connection to myself, and from the lighthouse that is my deep connection to art, ignoring the waves of intuition attempting to bring me back to safety, back to myself. At this point, there was only one thing left to do.

Chrissie stopped swimming, and Bruce got his next meal.

I have often thought that Art contains
the answers I've been searching for.

It whispers to me,
"Remember, wholeness is..."

Dance of the Nine Opals, Ithell Colquhoun. Part of the Ithell Colquhoun collection,
Tate Archive. Bequeathed by Ithell Colquhoun to the Tate Archive. © Tate.
Photo Credit: The Sherwin Collection, Leeds, UK/Bridgeman Images

PART TWO

Beneath the Surface

Wholeness is a sacred system.
Each part freely
expressing
the colors
of emotion flowing,
gently morphing,
welcoming the ensemble of self,
playing a symphony on strings of connectedness.
Working together—
towards deeper self-trust,
towards congruence,
towards relishing
the fullness of life.

You are enough here in the embrace of Art.

Peggy Lipschutz, *Wrested Heart*, 1999

Wrested Heart

Gently she studies
the glowing light of her heart
with love and patience

"You've got to get out of your own way" and "what got you here won't get you there" is the advice of every online business bro incessantly telling me how to 10x my business. There I was, burnt out and nursing my shark bites, with these exclamations from the seven-figure bro-marketers swimming confusedly around in my brain. I knew that not only could I not keep pushing and working my way through success as I have always done but that I needed to do something different and that I was the one standing in my own way. I was the problem. What does "get out of your own way" even mean? Even if I didn't really know what it meant, I still knew somehow that there was some truth to it. Or, at the very least, an exploration of what it meant would lead to something true.

I knew that there was something I was avoiding, and it wasn't a task I could check off my to-do list. I was avoiding thinking and feeling. Subconsciously, I was aware of the red flags and heard the ominous music playing beneath the surface, but I just wasn't ready to listen. Something in me knew that paying attention to those red flags meant blowing up what I had built. It meant stepping into some other version of me that I was afraid of becoming. I knew that doing this would mean I'd have to let go of things I wasn't ready to let go of. It meant I'd have to retrieve that chest I had sunk to the bottom of the ocean—the one that held my creativity and my heart. I would have to open it and really look inside at the heart I had buried to keep myself from sinking.

And the central figure in Peggy Lipschutz's *Wrested Heart* is doing just that. In the painting, a woman in a maroon dress sits on a bench in a dark, wooded place. Her dress peels open to reveal a gaping hole in her chest—hollow and empty. She holds her heart in her hands—hardened in a thick, stony shell. Her eyes look into a split in the rocky heart, a crack that opens the hard outer shell to reveal a glowing orange inside. The warm light reflects on her curious and loving gaze. As far as I had come in the decade before starting my business—healing my heart from shame and abandonment—I had started to lose connection with myself as the business and my drive for success took over. In the beginning, during the growing phase of my business, things seemed just as I pictured they would be. I was doing exciting work and making a difference in the world, but as the business grew, I abandoned some of the most important parts of myself in the name of growth and scale, namely my writing and my personal connection to art. Over time, that growth gave way to plateaued business results, just one symptom of something being out of alignment.

Starting my business was a turning point for me. It was a true act of self-trust and a deep connection with myself and what I wanted for my life, but in the growth of my business, that connection to myself grew weaker and weaker. My connection to art became more about my customers and less about myself. Whereas once in my life, I wrote poems as much as I made art and wrote pages and pages in my journal every day about my feelings, I had stopped writing altogether, not even able to write a few factual sentences. I realized that I could not ignore what haunted me beneath the surface. I was missing art, missing my spark, and missing the fun and excitement that my business once provided. I was missing a time when writing was free, expressive, and fun and not filled with anxiety and not-enoughness.

My voice felt utterly blocked, and I couldn't ignore it anymore.

I chose to begin this business with a big exciting goal (traveling around the world). I then took an inventory of my life, decided what needed to change, and worked full force to make those changes. I took a hard look at my external environment and saw where I was out of alignment with myself, even if I didn't yet know what "alignment" was. My environment clearly showed that I wasn't leading the life I wanted. So I changed my environment. But now? This was different. If I looked around at my life, I would see an environment that was just right. A successful business that makes a difference, enough money to feel comfortable and secure, a happy family, lots of fun with friends, and travel. But there was still something not right. But this time, it was something internal.

The answers could no longer be found outside me; I had to go beneath the surface. I had to open myself up.

✳ ✳ ✳

I started my journey with Picasso's *Girl Before A Mirror*—a girl looking at her reflection in the mirror and on the inside is pain, sadness, and anxiety. When I look at the girl outside of the mirror in Picasso's painting, the one looking into the mirror, I don't see a girl really trying to look inside and figure out the pain. The painful version of herself in the mirror is something to hide, something to be ashamed of, something repulsive, and something to avoid. The girl on the outside shows this with her agitated energy, her made-up face, and her firm grip on the sides of the mirror. Her face has no love, compassion, or curiosity like the woman in *Wrested Heart*. In *Wrested Heart*, the woman gently holds and protects her heart, and the forest is a cocoon holding space for her exploration.

All of the work I did to this point got me to a place where the girl on my inside is not something to be ashamed of, not something to be sad about, not something to bury, but someone to be curious about, someone to hold with compassion, and someone to be loved. When I met my daughters, I knew they were deeply loved and so deserving of it. There were no questions about that. But now, I allowed wonder and curiosity to come forth for myself. I asked myself the question that I had avoided for so long:

Who am I?

Who am I on the inside?

Now that the layers of shame have been removed...

Now that I am aware that there is something deeper within me, hiding behind all of the perfectionism and over-functioning,

Now that I have been forced to slow down,

Now that I had layers of support and love from my family and friends,

Now that I had the courage and the curiosity to start to let my true self show,

Now that I could look behind the veil of constant inner criticism...

Who am I?

Who am I *really*?

66 Of course I wake up finally thinking,
how wonderful to be who I am,
made out of earth and water,
my own thoughts, my own fingerprints—
all that glorious, temporary stuff. **99**

— Mary Oliver in "On Meditating, Sort Of" in *Devotions*

❉ ❉ ❉

I had felt safe enough to expand into the bigger life I wanted; I was at the top of Erik Johanson's stone staircase in *Grow with Progress* looking into the immensity of the horizon. And I'd like to say I looked beneath the surface because I felt safe enough to look inside and see myself, but actually, my shark friend, Bruce, forced me to look and make another change. Eventually, I came to a place where NOT looking inside was more detrimental to my being than anything else. I could no longer just continue to work hard and get where I wanted to go; that was no longer sustainable. I could no longer hide because the physical symptoms became too much to bear, and the business plateaued as I drifted further and further from my center. This burnout was a time to truly see what was inside. I had grown a business using other people's ideas and plans for implementation and lost the connection to myself. Now, I had to gently reconnect with myself, tap into my own wisdom, get in touch with my body and spirit, learn how to occupy this new life, and prepare myself to allow that unarmored, glowing heart to come back into my body.

Wrested Heart, a Poem

This light that burns within her
too big for her wounded spirit,
too powerful to be contained,
too precious to be shared,
too sacred to be understood.

This radiant love
so big
so full
She was scared it would break her
open,
too exposed,
too real.

Who is she to shine so brightly?
Who is she to contain such power?
Who is she to deserve such love?
Who is she to be so near the divine?

So she ripped the light from her chest,
breaking herself before she could be broken
                                        again
She encased it in a chest with steel locks.
Her finest treasure,
she buried it deep in the woods
without an X to mark its spot.

Yet...

its pulsing light continuing to glow
in the dark
in its armor
locked away but still
alive

They say time heals all wounds,
but the chasm in her chest remained
open and tender.

Cold.

Forgetting the presence of the light
longing for its remembered warmth,
she searched for ways to become
whole again.

While slowly beneath the forest floor,
warmth decays the leaves into damp soil,
fungi thread around the light to carry its message,
worms burrow up to its mysterious heat,
seeds sprout, and flowers bloom.
Her deserted light inspires
life and vitality

Even forgotten, the abandoned light
still burns.
Locked away,
it still burns.
Fueled by an infinite source,
it still burns.

This life-giving light is safe
protected in the cocoon
of the quiet forest
Yet it does not belong.

It burns for her.
It waits for her.
It belongs
with her.

It calls to her,
sending its light
through the soul of the forest
as a beacon,
beckoning her

Return.

Remember.

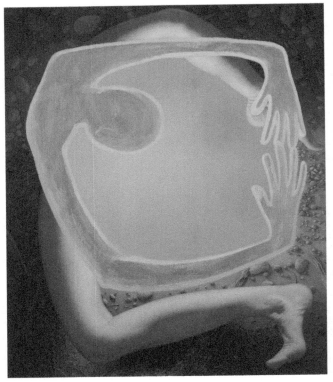

Aleah Chapin, *The Opening*, 2020-21
Image courtesy of the artist and Flowers Gallery

The Opening

Grasping, struggling,
Can't hold it in anymore.
Let emotions flow.

What's left?

What's left
when you remove
expectations of being
the smartest
the most impressive
the most put-together
the most thoughtful
the kindest
the meekest
the one who makes no waves
causes no inconveniences

What's left
when you're done
contorting
squeezing
to fit in places
you never even wanted to be

when you remove
co-opted identities
that never sat right in your skin

What's left
when your body starts to become
unrecognizable
when you feel flat
drawn
empty
two-dimensional

Passing as an acceptable
facade of a person
not contoured and robust
not whole

What's left
when you're bare
on the barren ground
not sure
if you ever knew
yourself

What's left
when you are
s t r e t c h e d
so thin
trying to hold
expectations that you cannot
bear to hold
anymore

What's left
when you are gripping
so tight
that you ache
and shake
muscles so tense
they beg

Let go.

Hold It In

Stay steady, she says
Tears well up
Zip it up, she says
Don't let the pain show
Pain from holding in
truth and tears

If you cry
You will be shut out
You will be left
You will be
abandoned
Alone
sitting on the ground
surrounded by your baggage
digging
searching
Find a way to fix it
before they drive away
leaving you alone
again

Your baggage is too heavy
Your emotions are too much
You are too much

And you are your own
problem
Unseen
Unsupported
Invisible

Just relax
Don't cry
Hold in your fear
Smile so they hear
it in your voice

Hold the Wind

Hold on
to the wind,
brace yourself,
tensing, panicking,
holding strong,
a quick inhale and a catch,
stay still to keep the breath in

Hold the wind
in the pink space of dawn,
swishing
in the embrace of my arms,
wind unruly in the canyon
its dust cloud obscuring thought

Hold the wind,
sound whooshing and washing my mind
allow the swirl to clean out
the last remnants
of old shame,
the energy of past pain

Release the wind
release the tension,
let the pain be carried away
lay down, let go
lay down, spread limbs flat to the ground

Release the wind
Release the tension to the earth
Release the breath I've been holding for so long

Exhale
around and around and out
allow the wholeness that is already here

I am real

I Belong to Myself

I may be an embodiment of the patriarchy's failure—not being able to be small, to stay small, to keep myself zipped up. Not being able to hold in my BIGness.

But I am not a failure to myself.

I have been here for myself, for all of my everythings. I have made it through with no models of how to be a whole human being—real and raw. Vulnerable. Not just one who acts whole, but who embodies whole. One who is not afraid of herself. One knows there is no broken.

There is no broken.

I found wholeness even when wholeness didn't seem possible.

I have moved through the world my whole life intuitively knowing "it's not okay."
It's not okay to live in a world where we have to lock our true selves inside just to feel like we belong.
It's not okay to not show love and be love for your loved ones.
It's not okay to not honor the humanity and emotions of each other.
It's not okay to live with sadness and anxiety and depression alone.
It's not okay to love conditionally.

It's not okay to abandon yourself.

I have not abandoned myself. I always come back home to who I am at my core. This loving, emotional, full, pulsing, energetic, heart-filled person. Full, free, unzipped, unrestrained.

My heart is big and full and strong and I didn't know it. Until now.

Now I know I belong to myself and that is enough.

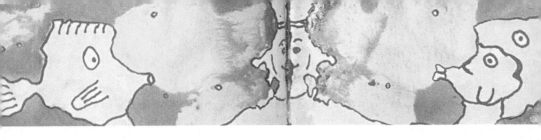

Natalie Wadlington, *Night*, 2022. Photo by Kevin Todora.
Image courtesy of the artist and Library Street Collective

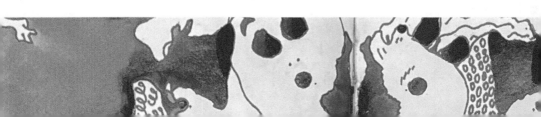

Night

Curious at peace
Safe in the world she creates
Full and embodied

In 2019, I realized that the shark had gotten me, that I was over-whelmed, burnt out, and not having fun anymore in my business. I felt so burdened and so weighed down. I could sense my feelings living just beneath my skin, waiting to be felt, but I didn't know exactly how to do that after a lifetime of stuffing those feelings down. I started working with a coach, Lisa Carpenter, who helps over-functioning women return to their bodies, emotions, and well-being. Immediately upon working with her, I looked at my life and started drastically slashing the things weighing me down. I canceled two of the three intensive business groups I was in and stopped attending the third. And I added in healthcare practitioners and healers. It was time to start peeling back the layers, looking inside myself with compassion and curiosity. I hadn't felt good in a long time, and I desperately wanted to feel good.

One of the experiences I added was hypnotherapy. I booked a package of six two-hour sessions with an incredible hypnotherapist, Penny Chiasson, to help identify the root of my healing inside my subconscious. I had dabbled in self-hypnosis recordings in the prior year and knew its power. What happened in those six sessions was profound but fuzzy in my memory. I brought a feeling of being burdened to these sessions, and the feeling we focused on cultivating in our time together was freedom and ease in my body, emotions, and spirit. In each session, she had me visualize myself in this free state. I always saw a vision of me smiling and talking excitedly, feeling light and happy, not questioning all of my movements, and just being present.

In the sessions focusing on feelings, she led me through tunnels back in time to memories. The two memories that came up that I still remember from the hypnosis were minor things, not sure they were even real, but one of them, I was maybe ten years old, standing outside of my house nervously waiting for someone to come out—I was about to get in trouble. And the second was me in a playpen—probably two or three years old at the oldest because I was wearing a diaper—in the living room of one of our early houses. Again, in this memory, I expectantly wait for the door to open and something bad to happen. It fascinated me that these "memories" (whether or not they were real memories) were not bad things actually happening but me in a state of fear as if something terrible was about to happen. For someone who is coming in burdened and wanting to feel free, you can imagine how much of a burden that anticipatory fear was on my system.

After exploring these memories, we tunneled into the womb. I'm not saying I actually remember being in the womb, but in the visualizations, I did imagine myself there. Talking about the feelings in each of the memories and situations that came up, I described the emotions I felt to my hypnotherapist as we went. Then we spent some time exploring what I wanted each of those young versions of me to know—that she is safe, that her pain has ended, that now in the future she can be free, that she has me to support her, love her, and be with her. And also at some point in the sessions, we focused on my bio-dad. In the hypnosis, I imagined sitting across from him and telling him everything I needed to say.

After rooting in the new knowledge of my growth and healing, we tunneled forward in time to each of the memories that had come up. I comforted that young version of me. I held her and was with her. I told her she was safe. I gave her what she needed. I parented her in the ways she yearned to be parented. I felt differently at the end of the six sessions but couldn't articulate what had changed. I knew the power of what I had experienced but that I wouldn't necessarily see its impact until later. People would ask if I recommended it and how it was, and I would tell them, "I don't know how to describe it, but yes, I feel different. Something is vastly different, and I just don't know what it is or how to talk about it right now."

Well, now is later. When writing this book, I was trying to articulate what allowed me to look back at my past, myself, my bio-dad, and my mom, with such compassion when it used to be filled with shame, resentment, anger, pain, or sadness. All of the healing, therapy, coaching, reading, and work on myself that I have done has contributed, but I think I underestimated the impact of that hypnosis experience. I almost completely forgot about it. Since that experience,

I have been able to reconnect with who I really am with love and compassion.

I see that sad little girl, but I also see how funny, quirky, and excited she was about things.

I see her curiosity, wonder, inquisitiveness, and inventiveness. A girl who is never really alone because she always has the vastness of her imagination and creativity inside her head.

> **"** How I picture it: We are all nesting dolls, carrying the earlier iterations of ourselves inside. We carry the past inside us. We take ourselves —all of ourselves—wherever we go. **"**
> — Maggie Smith in *You Could Make This Place Beautiful*

✳ ✳ ✳

At the same time I was reconnecting with myself and my childhood, I visited an incredible exhibit at the Dallas Contemporary, *Places That Grow* by Natalie Wadlington. The galleries of my favorite Dallas museum were filled with massive, bright-colored canvases—each featuring a young girl as the protagonist. (I am gendering her as a young girl as the artist and I are both female, and I am putting myself into these paintings, but there is nothing other than her long hair that tells me she is a girl in the actual paintings.) In most of Wadlington's paintings, the girl was outside, engaging with the world—inspecting insects of varying sorts, playing with her dog, gardening, or pulling weeds. After exploring the exhibit, I decided to choose one of the paintings I felt most connected to and spend more time with it. I decided to sit in front of *Night* by Natalie Wadlington.

In the painting, the girl sits in her backyard at night. She sits contortedly on plush grass as she shines a flashlight on two ants crawling on the bottom of her bare foot. Her wide-eyed, curious expression shows that she is fascinated by these ants, analyzing their behavior in wonder. This backyard scene is so peaceful. Stars and a full moon light up the night sky. Around her backyard are a trickling water feature, a fire pit crackling and glowing with two chairs beside it, and a shell-encrusted water fountain showing a fish with an open mouth surrounded by rose bushes. Three bejeweled paver stones showing her handprints through time cut up through the center towards a tree. A harmless garden snake slithers across a sidewalk toward the girl's shoes.

If you had asked me before the hypnosis, before I learned to slow down and feel my feelings, I would have told you about the sad Cindy, crying every night, longing for her dad, wondering why he left her. She had too many feelings about too many things and nowhere and no one to turn to who knew how to handle such strong emotions. But by healing myself and removing the layers of shame, I started to see myself and who I am. When I look back, I can see the comfort, too. The creativity and the inventiveness and the curiosity. The humor and the giggle (a giggle I still get comments about, so I'm grateful for the mute button on Zoom so the soundtrack of all my meetings isn't my incessant giggle).

Before, what made me different and what made me stand out were things my surroundings told me I should be ashamed of. I had developed this need to constantly be pushing forward to escape who I was—a continuous forward motion, a non-stop wishing for any circumstantial thing to take me out of my pain, moving to a new place, a new job, a new life. When I slowed down, the anxiety came. When I would sit and rest on a weekend, layers of guilt and shame tormented and engulfed me. I felt guilty because I grew up in a house (and a whole culture) focused on productivity and getting things done. I don't think this was unique. This mindset is still prevalent. If there is housework to do and you aren't doing it, you are lazy and should feel guilty. I have ADHD and have always struggled with productivity (but was undiagnosed until 2022). My mind races with possibility and energy, and I feel good when those synapses are firing. The idea of sitting peacefully in the grass was hard to imagine, until I tried it.

In the last year, I've ventured more and more into the trying. One of these adventures was a retreat led by my colleague Angie Stegall. She guided us through an activity called Forest Bathing. I was amazed at this experience because it is so much like what I do with people with art, but it was with nature. We strolled at a snail's pace through the woods in Pisgah National Forest in North Carolina, doing various activities like singling out our senses, paying attention to all the movement around us, and making a frame out of sticks on the ground to focus on the small details in the rich soil. It was a magical experience to be that present in nature and with myself and others, slowing down, being raw and vulnerable, stripped of technology and comfort, with only who we are and what the earth has to offer. The first night was miserable and snowy, but when we were forest bathing, the sun came out, and I lay on the ground in the woods and felt the warmth on my skin after a rough night. It felt sacred and special—not unlike my trips to the art museum.

At one point, we were focused on textures, and I crouched near the trickle of a stream and ran my hands through the cold, crystal water. Suddenly, I noticed I was in the same signature crouch as my daughter Zoey when she does similar activities, and all at once I became both my daughter and my current self. I also time-warped to my childhood—remembering I used to be the same way. I became little Cindy, delighting in nature in her backyard. In one moment, I was past, present, and future. It was a place of peace, compassion, and understanding. No shame or sadness, just seeing myself, who I was, who I became, and who I created so clearly I started to cry.

This painting fills me with such a feeling of peace and presence. It's massive—eight and a half feet square. It completely engulfs the viewer and places them in this beautiful moment of a familiar yet otherworldly scene. A scene that in my past would have made me supremely uncomfortable. If I had seen this art at another time—the time before, let's call it—it would have made me squirm to be in such peace. I know I would have wanted to escape. I'm speculating here, it's just a guess, but I think this art would have brought up so much discomfort that I would have struggled. In the time since the time before, so much has changed. I have cultivated a tolerance for being in my feelings, and now this painting is like coming home to myself. I see myself in it so clearly, and I also see my daughter, Zoey.

If seeing myself in *Night* was clear to me, finding Zoey there felt like magic. This painting is Zoey. Zoey has always loved to squat down and play in nature. I have this crystal clear vision of her, crouched in a ball, her hands drawing circles in the dirt, making stacks of leaves, digging for rocks and gems, or swishing her hand through water. If you watch her, she is entirely in her own world, rapt with her discoveries. She isn't narrating it like my other daughter would do or wanting to photograph it to remember or googling science things like I would be doing. She is lost in the delight and presence of the moment.

❝ I hadn't counted on the circularity of life: the way it delivers us, with age, back to the beginning. ❞
— Jennifer Egan in *The Candy House*

✳ ✳ ✳

I forget where I heard this, but someone once told me that we have three opportunities to be parented—one by our actual parents, once as we parent our own children if we have them, and then as we reparent ourselves, giving ourselves what we needed when we were kids. The hypnosis and the work I have done over the years have allowed me to provide myself with what I always needed as a child:

validating my emotions,

celebrating who I am as I am,

building up my self-esteem,

knowing I was loved no matter what and that I wouldn't be abandoned,

showing me that love is unconditional, that I don't have to be productive or busy or a certain size,

learning about my sensitivities, my introversion, my anxiety, my neurodivergence.

My self-development work has given me all these things, but so has art. Being with art allows me to have hard conversations and not skirt around my wants and needs. When I allow myself to be with this piece in particular, I am instantly transported back to that powerful experience in the woods when I saw this painting. I feel the essence of the honesty and clear communication I have brought into my life. I see myself now, myself then, and my daughter in the girl in the picture. Once I learned I could be with myself, I could also see myself in the girl in *Night*. I look at this girl, and she is an embodiment of me. I could feel her curiosity and her ability to become absorbed in the present moment. Her ability became my ability. Getting out of my head and into my body, into the present environment. That's what art does. It allows you to expand and recognize yourself in a place that may have seemed forbidden, irresponsible, or unattainable.

She is contorted, twisting, and stretching her body to get a better look at the ants. She is comfortable in her body even though this position looks uncomfortable. Her discomfort is embraced, not registering as discomfort; she has the wherewithal to navigate the discomfort because she is experiencing awe, curiosity, and specialness. She is safe in her body, and her body is providing her the space to live this life.

Her twistiness shows her flexibility too. I used to be so rigid; I thought I had to be a certain way to be an adult. Everything was black and white, right or wrong. But in the after time, I have a different view. I can see all sides, and I can understand different perspectives. This person I have become has psychological flexibility, which is "the open acceptance of unpleasant sensations, thoughts, and feelings, while focusing on the present moment" (Ramaci et al., 2019). This psychological flexibility is my friend and helps me navigate the places in which I feel I need to change to be welcomed. I see my value and the value of my curiosity and specialness.

There's more in this painting for me, too. Looking deeper, I see her presence and mindfulness in this moment. Her mind isn't getting hooked on the stories she is telling herself about her emotions, body, or life. She is 100 percent present and there for herself and with herself. The stones show the passage of time; she is happy where she is, each year becoming more and more herself.

I see her wide eyes and open mouth. I see her brain existing in a state of wonder and awe. Once upon a time, my awe once was a thing that I was embarrassed by. I learned somewhere along the way that my excitement and the things I am excited about overwhelm people, and after the overwhelm comes judgment, eye rolls, or impatient sighs. The girl in the painting is not awaiting an eye roll or looking over her shoulder, embarrassed that she is so entranced by these ants. She is letting them enrapture her. She is choosing delight and wonder. She is seeing her place in the massive world with so many things to be in awe of, from the tiny ants to the starry universe and full moon. She has surrendered to her awe, letting it contort her body into an uncomfortable position to get a better look at her curiosity.

66 There is ecstasy in paying attention. 99
— Anne Lamott in *Bird by Bird*

Safe in her space, she exists in a state of possibility and the expansiveness of the night sky. She doesn't long to be somewhere else. She can experience the expansiveness of life anywhere, even in her backyard.

She exists here in this huge painting that captures the wholeness of her being.

It holds her as she is.

Within her, she has a crackling fire and passion.

Within her, she has a welcoming seat for the parts of her that need attention.

She welcomes others into her heart too.

Knowing that she is capable of being loved and of loving.

Knowing she has the gift for holding space and creating connection.

Knowing that allowing herself to be in her wholeness shows others how to be the same.

Within her, sure there are cracks on the sidewalk and things to work on and things she wants to change, but those parts are welcome along with the awe and the curiosity. In the quiet stillness of her wholeness, she has emotions. A snake of guilt, grief, or insecurity slithers in, but it is welcome. It isn't a threat or a place of panic. She has ants that crawl on her skin, which could be a threat, could make her squirm, they could bite her and leave a mark, but she welcomes them in too. She is curious about them and their behavior. She wants to learn more so they can peacefully coexist.

In her wholeness, she is not just her intelligence. She is her physical body, her energy, her emotions, and her spirit. In *The Language of Emotions*, Karla McLaren compares all of these parts of people with the elements—water being emotions, earth being the body, air being the intellect, and fire being the spirit/energy. All of these elements are represented in the painting. The emotions flow through the three-tiered water fountain. The fire crackles in the firepit, burns as stars in the sky, and shows the vastness and warmth of her energy. The air is all around her. The lush earth holding her whole being.

In her wholeness, she sees the imprints of who she was in the past and creates a path to who she is now and where she is going. She can take off the shoes of her daily concerns and worries and sit in the plush grass. She has created a path for herself that leads up through time with space for the next stone, the next handprint. But no matter where it leads, she still belongs to herself, and she is still safe with herself.

What if I am held just as I am?

What if I don't need to be fixed?

What if I am whole and unbroken?

What if I have always been whole and unbroken?

What if, when I am alone, I am not lonely?

What if I can wander within myself just like this girl?

What if my wandering leads me to wholeness?

That's what I see when I look at this painting: wholeness. The fullness of it, the safety of it, the comfort of it, the expansiveness of it.

Marcos Raya, *The Anguish of Being and the Nothingness of the Universe*, 2000,
Acrylic on canvas, Diameter: 69 ½ in. (176.5 cm), The Museum of Fine Arts, Houston,
Museum purchase funded by Roy Cullen in honor of Mary Cullen at "One Great Night
in November, 2005", 2005.1070 © Marcos Raya Photo Copyright:
Photograph © The Museum of Fine Arts, Houston; Thomas R. DuBrock

The Anguish of Being and the Nothingness of the Universe

Seeing through his eyes,
wandering alone, unknown,
I find compassion.

Mr. Rogers said, "You can't really love someone else unless you really love yourself first." While I don't think that's particularly true or helpful, especially for those who have been through traumatic experiences, I think coming to a place where I felt I was worthy of love is a thread I have followed through this healing journey. When I met my friends and found a home in their embrace, I decided to suspend my disbelief and pretend that I was likable and worthy of love. And in that place of pretending I was loved, a shift happened; somewhere along the way, I didn't have to pretend anymore. I could believe I was lovable, and therefore I could start to actually receive the love others had tried to give me for all those years. (And just for the record, my husband and family loved me through all this, even though I didn't love myself.)

One of the places I learned how to receive and give love was in my friendship with my dear friend, Madalyn. I met her when our babies were both babies. Our friendship blossomed over the years as we realized that we shared so many of the same values and heart, getting closer and closer until she eventually started working for me at Art Class Curator.

She began making transcripts of my art teacher trainings, and eventually, I realized I needed her as my full-time project manager. When you have a lifetime of trust issues and create a business that is an extension of you, it's hard to find someone that you can trust with your creation. With Madalyn, though, it was easy.

Madalyn became an integral part of my days and my life, and we'd talk to each other all day, every day. Sometimes it was work-related—deep conversations about art and what it means to us—and then other times, we had hours of Voxer conversations debating whether or not we would want to live forever. She taught me that there was a place for my excitement over things that elicited eye rolls from others; what I found in my relationship with Madalyn was that she was just as excited as me. Watching her arms flail in the air with excitement at a mention of her favorite book in trivia or crying together in front of a painting that we both profoundly connected with, I have someone by my side who provides a loving and safe container in which we both can grow in support of one another.

In our conversations, I started to discover a deeper philosophy of art. That art, for me, was more than just learning about art history or appreciating something beautiful. It was with her that I developed the capacity and the courage to make the conversation about something else. As I started exploring this new direction in my thought and business, Madalyn and I began discussing art on my podcast. The podcast had been running for a few years; mostly, it was a vehicle to tell people about the power of art, telling telling telling, but not giving space for showing them the possibility art holds on a personal level. Then, in a moment of connectedness, I had the idea to bring Madalyn onto my podcast. But this time, I would put up a juicy work of art that we both love and let the conversation flow wherever it might go—to show everyone the magic in my conversations with Madalyn behind the scenes. It was with her that I learned that I had ideas worth listening to and stories worth telling, and I know if it weren't for her loving presence in my life, you might not be reading this book right now.

It was during one of these magical podcast discussions when I made a startling revelation that an artwork I had seen and worked with for years had a direct and powerful connection to my biological dad. About forty-five minutes into the episode about *The Anguish of Being and the Nothingness of the Universe* by Marcos Raya, I stopped in my tracks—seeing his face in the artwork clear as day. I mean, I had seen this artwork again and again over many, many months because it is included in lesson plans for Art Class Curator. I even have a selfie of me with it at the Museum of Fine Arts Houston, but that was in those "just keep swimming" days when art became more about a business task and less about uncovering my heart and soul.

I didn't realize until I was in that conversation with Madalyn what magic there was for me in this painting—reminding me once again of the power of discussing art but also the magic of the art hitting you differently depending on where you are in your life and also who you were with. I was in the safe space of my container with Madalyn. And emotionally, I wasn't ready for that connection to be made before, and then I was.

※ ※ ※

The painting is hard to describe because it is unlike anything I have seen. It is a tondo which is a fancy way of saying it is round. It's large, with a diameter of almost six feet, and at the museum, it's hung high on the wall, so you have to look up at it to enjoy its vastness, which makes it seem even bigger. The painting depicts what looks to be the interior of a mask of an abstracted face—almost like a robotic mask, but alive and immersed in pain. The eyes are empty openings in the shape of aviator glasses filled with stars and galaxies. Through the gaps and along the side of the face, we see more of the infinite night sky beyond the face.

The abstracted inside of the face looks mechanical—tubular, striped in places, and stitched together with small bone shapes and fragile lines. The edges of the mask resemble cardboard—adding to this sense of fragility. The bones, if you can call them that, above the mouth are stitched together with small threads, and three teeth are missing from an otherwise complete set. The colors are disconcerting and clashing—orange in displeasing gradation with green, light pink and blue, black, and white.

Looking at the painting, I feel as if I am looking into the world through this person's eyes. The missing teeth, the deconstruction, and the clashing colors made Madalyn and I feel like this figure was in pain. We both felt a sense of unease as we looked at the painting, not knowing why, so it made even more sense to me why I hadn't fully engaged with it more deeply before. Something is disturbing about this artwork; the whole time Madalyn and I talked about it, I felt that tension. Usually in our art conversations, we revel in the delight of experiencing the artwork, but we remarked that it made us increasingly uncomfortable this time. We were finding it almost a little hard to look at for an extended period of time.

In our podcast, Madalyn and I talked about what it meant to look through someone else's eyes, how the work reflects the messiness and complexity of life and space, how the painting puts the mundane of day-to-day life in perspective, and the contrast between the sterile cleanliness of the painting and the message it conveys. Just as I started to feel more at ease with the artwork and the rhythm of discussing it and finding mean-ing, I suddenly realized an intense personal connection to this artwork that stopped me cold.

It became apparent in the process of looking through the empty eyes of this strange figure that I was looking through the eyes of my alcoholic biological father. I probably should have noticed this connection earlier because the museum label text of the artwork discusses the artist's battle with alcoholism, but to be honest I usually don't spend too much time thinking about what is written on labels. I suppose I wasn't ready for this connection until I found it myself. I was at a place of healing about my childhood experience and with my bio-dad, catalyzed by that powerful hypnosis. In this rediscovery of my childhood, I found more compassion, connection, and curiosity for myself. Now it seemed that compassion, connection, and curiosity could now be focused towards my bio-dad instead of resentment, anger, pity, and sadness.

✻ ✻ ✻

As you know, my biological dad was an alcoholic, but there is more to this art connection than alcoholism alone. After those formative years of crying every night after he left, there's a little more to the story. He returned to my life a few times, reopening those sad wounds that slowly started to harden into anger and armor. The first time I heard from him was on my twelfth birthday, about three years after he left. He called out of the blue—saying he missed me and wished me a happy birthday. I can't remember his exact words because the immediate flood of emotions took control of my nervous system—blocking out everything but emotion and sensation. Just when I felt like I was starting to move on, his call reopened that gaping hole in my heart and sent me into a day of tears. Once the sadness subsided, my anger took hold and didn't let up for a long time. After all the leaving and the tears and the hurt, he ruined my birthday (a twelve-year-old's birthday is a BIG deal).

But that call also triggered something in me—a knowing that he still existed, remembered me, and maybe loved me. In the back of my head, that thought lingered and nagged at me, getting louder and louder as the months and years passed. The curiosity about where he was and why he ruined my childhood grew bigger and bigger until it started to torment me (I don't believe now he destroyed my childhood, but at the time in my hormonal adolescent body, I for sure thought that). I wanted to see him again. I needed to see him again to get some closure, answers, and a better understanding of what happened when I was a child. I couldn't take the uncertainty anymore. I couldn't take the not knowing. So in my first year of high school, I finally opened up to my sister Jenny, then in her senior year, about this growing, nagging desire.

Jenny and I were both raised in the same house, with the same parents, and in the same situations. We both had similar trauma. Still, her being older, the instability of the alcoholism and frequent moving played a more prominent role, while the abandonment was my biggest trauma. But we both have the same mom, who focuses on the present and doesn't show her own emotions often.

In this atmosphere, it still surprises me that I went to my sister for help. It wasn't an easy decision to make at that time. I have no memory of ever before this honestly talking about our shared trauma. I felt wholly alone in my feelings, as I am sure she was alone in hers. We had no models for how to be there for each other through this or process what had happened to us. But she was the closest person to me who had also experienced this loss, and so, as difficult as it was, I went to her for help. (I still struggle with this—going up to someone with something so big and saying, "I need help.") When I went to her, I was allowing myself to be seen. In my mind, anytime I asked for help was admitting failure. It was admitting weakness. It acknowledged that I didn't have it together as much as I pretended. I fearfully ruminated about coming to her for a while before I finally got the words out.

I'm sad.

I'm struggling.

I need help.

I don't know what to do.

Like me, Jenny's a take-charge type of person. She swung into action, and we sought him out. I don't exactly remember the details. I wish I did, but the truth is that some protective part of me immediately shut this out of my memory. I have flashes of being in Jenny's car, following up on possible places and leads we had after calling some of his family members. We eventually found him and met up with him after many years apart.

I don't remember what we said, where we went, or what we did, but his appearance is burned in my memory. He looked tired, sad, and older than his actual age. Although brushed and neat, his hair looked a little too long for his balding head, but the most prominent feature I noticed was that several of his teeth were missing. Anytime I picture him now, those missing teeth are the first thing I think of, so it is a surprise to me that it took me so long to make the connection to the missing teeth in Marcos Raya's artwork. In my mind's eye, his form is a compilation of both photos and the hazy memories of him in person. I saw this mental picture reflected back at me in the artwork. In that mental picture, he wears those classic, gold wire-rimmed glasses with the wire that goes across the top, popular in the '70s and '80s—very similar in style to the aviator glasses of the figure in the artwork.

But beyond the teeth and the glasses, the painting matches the overall impression I got of him that day too—the raw discomfort, the tension, the unease, the fragile stitched-together insides, and the overall grimace of a hard life lived with infinite regrets (or so I assume and more uncomfortable to admit, hope). Although we didn't know it then, he was only ten years from his impending death. I can't imagine what these regrets did to him, nor did I even attempt to try until after I connected with Raya's artwork, but in my mental image of him, he seems to be just a shell of a person hiding behind a mask, just existing in his pain. The artwork's title, *The Anguish of Being and the Nothingness of the Universe*, fits exactly this image I have of him. His anguish is clear, and as a hurt and indignant teen, I didn't yet have compassion or understanding for him and his experience of the events of his life. I couldn't honor his humanity.

Seeing him once led to us seeing him a few more times, sharing a few meals at local restaurants. Although I don't remember what we said, I do remember feeling closed off, protecting my armored heart, but in the end, this new budding relationship between him and me fizzled. I was done. The nagging to have him in my life stopped, and I saw him as a sad stranger, not the dad I remember loving so fiercely. He sent me occasional letters and emails once computers were on the scene after these meetups, but I always interpreted them as a guilt trip for me not wanting to see him anymore and for changing my last name to my stepdad's. That old anger was still holding tight. I thought it ironic that he somehow blamed me for the fizzle of our newly-engaged relationship when he was the one who did the leaving in the first place.

Once my sister Jenny went off to college, she kept seeing him semi-regularly as he drove through her college town for his traveling pharmaceutical sales job, mostly out of pity for him, she says. I had no interest at that point. He had hurt me enough, and I wouldn't allow myself to be hurt any longer by him.

✳ ✳ ✳

In 2005 my bio-dad died, and I didn't shed a tear. I was sitting around the dining table in my childhood home playing Scrabble® with my mom and sister over Christmas break when we got that call. Bio-dad had died of a heart attack, and we just kept playing. No reaction. It was just nothingness. Like learning a celebrity died that you saw in a movie once. That wall over my heart was impenetrable. I didn't feel anything. My aunt, his sister, told us of the funeral plans, but Jenny and I weren't interested. I didn't go to his funeral. I honestly had no desire to. The walls of my heart were too thick. And although he had such a looming presence in my childhood memories, the anguish hiding behind his stitched-together mask was a mystery to me.

As I became an adult, I started to realize and learn about what alcoholism really is. It's a disease I'd always hear people say (as I listened with not a small degree of skepticism). Alcoholics don't have any control over it, and their addiction overpowers their relationships and responsibilities. When I heard public figures speak about their addictions, the truth of this seemed real. I could empathize in a way with the addicts in those stories, but in bio-dad, my anger would not allow me to forgive him.

My anger and sadness would not let me see his humanity, his anguish, and the struggles hiding behind the mask he wore. I could only see his behavior: what he did to me and what he did to my mom and my sister. He chose alcohol over his children. I could never forgive that.

❄ ❄ ❄

Twenty years later, I started to wonder about him again. As I healed with therapy, hypnosis, theta healing, coaching, and all the things, I began to dismantle that armor I built around my heart, piece by piece. It turns out those attachment wounds from childhood are not only lasting but also tricky. I spent countless hours consoling that young version of me, being that strong, loving, unconditional presence that she had needed.

I healed by making friends who taught me that I was not easy to leave and that I was lovable. They wanted me around. I was not a burden.

I healed by listening to and trusting my intuition.

I healed by starting to stand up for myself instead of people-pleasing all the time.

I healed by celebrating what made me different rather than being ashamed of my uniqueness.

And as I healed, I became less afraid of myself and others. I found love and acceptance both from others and, most importantly, from myself. I removed my mask, deciding to leave the hiding in the past.

Healing from my trauma allowed me to look back at my bio-dad situation with a new perspective—with curiosity and budding compassion rather than sadness and resentment for a lost childhood. I started to be able to talk about his behavior and my experience without crying.

As a coping mechanism, I had become committed to the story that the hardships in my childhood somehow made me stronger. I started dismantling that story too. That story built up the wall, and not until I saw myself as that little sad girl who needed love and didn't deserve what happened to her could I fully heal. I saw her, and I comforted her.

When I became a mom in 2009, I experienced firsthand a parent's overwhelming love and protective instincts. I realized you must have some pretty big demons if it trumps your love for your kids. You would think having kids would make what he did worse, but somehow it made me see the hold of the alcohol even stronger. It made me remember feeling loved by him. You hear of parents mistreating their children, neglecting them, and not showing them love. But I do remember his love, and I can still feel it now. The addiction must have been pretty bad to eclipse that love. And perhaps those fragile stitches in the mask in *The Anguish of Being* were the love that was holding him together. It wasn't strong enough, though, to fight his addictions and his unknown traumas.

> **"** I had roads to travel before I would know it's not that simple, the dope versus the person you love. That a craving can ratchet itself up and up inside a body and mind, at the same time that body's strength for tolerating its favorite drug goes down and down. **"**
> — Barbara Kingsolver in *Demon Copperhead*

When my daughters became the ages I was when bio-dad disappeared, I healed even more by giving them the love, connection, and understanding that I needed when I was their age, and I healed as I witnessed them be fiercely loved by their dad, my husband. Tears well up when I see him give them big bear hugs, play video games, or talk to them about their feelings. To imagine my daughters with the pain I suffered breaks me into a million pieces. And yet, my love for them is strong enough to piece me back together and make me whole.

I sometimes have difficulty separating them from me—seeing them as little versions of me, with all the sadness, self-esteem issues, and anxieties I experienced. I watch them intensely sometimes, looking for signs of what I experienced—making sure I don't miss any of the signs that were missed in me. It pleasantly surprises me when I realize they are not me. I try not to burden them with my baggage and remind myself regularly that they are individuals with their own struggles, pain, and sadness. I want to keep all the pain of the world away from them and give them what I didn't have, which is impossible. But I can love them and be that strong and unconditional presence that they need.

It's interesting to look back and realize that I only knew bio-dad from one perspective—the view of a sad child looking up to the man she loved.

But really, he was a sad man behind a mask like in *The Anguish of Being*, hiding the pain underneath. As I started to see elements of my personality in my daughters as they have grown—Lily's creativity, sense of humor, musical theater obsession, and love of office supplies and Zoey's giant heart, commitment to excellence, passionate interests, and competitive spirit, I started to wonder what elements of bio-dad are in me.

Was he also a deep feeler and highly intuitive? Was the world just slightly too loud and overwhelming for him like it is for me? Instead of turning to self-development books, cocoons of pillows and blankets, video games, food, and art like I did, did he turn to poisonous substances to turn down the dial on the world? What happened to him in his life that led to this? How did his Air Force deployment in the Vietnam War impact his alcoholism, potential PTSD, and connection with the world? Did he ever have anyone to talk to—anyone to help him, or did he push everyone away? How did his love for me feel? Was he filled with regret, sadness, or anger when he thought about me? What universe did he see through those aviator glasses?

Ultimately these are questions to which I will never know the answer. He is gone, and my mom refuses to relive her painful past by answering questions about what he was like. I don't blame her. Even if she did talk about her experience with him, her memories would only be part of the story—one-sided. But looking through the eyes of Marcos Raya's haunting figure, I realize the connection to my father is still available to me. I see him more clearly than I ever have. I see his stitched-together parts and his pain, and I see him wondering about the same vast universe that I love to wonder about.

I think my dad did experience nothing but *"the anguish of being,"* and when he looked into the sky, both the pain he felt and the pain that he caused his family must have felt overwhelming and disconnected. He drowned that anguish in alcohol and stuffed down his despair. I hope he knows that after my first forty-two years of floundering through life, working on myself one day at a time, one emotion at a time, I relish in *"the anguish of being"* rather than run from it or numb from it. I've embraced the agony and the ecstasy of life. My emotions are wide and varied and show that I am alive.

When I look into the vastness of space, I don't see *"the nothingness of the universe."* It doesn't make me feel small; it makes me feel like a miracle. I see its everythingness—that the complex world inside of me is multiplied into infinity by every other person, being, planet, solar system, galaxy, and beyond. I see that I am a part of it all, and it is a part of me. My dad and I will eventually be stardust together that some other being in some different galaxy will also wonder about—seeing themselves as part of it all too. The art, Marcos Raya's experience with alcoholism, and his expression of that experience connect me to the artist and his experience, to my inner child, to my dead father, to the vastness of the universe, and ultimately back to myself.

✳ ✳ ✳

After this deeper understanding of anguish and nothingness, I visited the Crow Museum of Asian Art in Dallas, where there was an installation called *River of Time* by Pamela Nelson. The artwork consists of hundreds of woven-together ribbons. On each ribbon, visitors were invited to write the names of loved ones they've lost, along with messages to the departed. In the installation, Nelson wove all of the patron's ribbons into a huge undulating tapestry of whites, blues, and greens coming from the ceiling like a waterfall and winding along the gallery floor like a river. The artist compared grief to a river saying:

> **66** [Grief] always keeps changing and always keeps moving, but goes in one direction—toward healing. **99**
> — Pamela Nelson

A pile of ribbons lay on the table for the art museum visitors to write their own messages to be woven into the collected river of grief at regular intervals by the artist. Standing before the pile of ribbons, I thought about what I would want to tell my bio-dad if I could tell him anything. I don't understand forgiveness yet—that's something I need to reflect on, so I couldn't tell him he was forgiven. I still don't know what that means in this situation. I didn't want to ask more questions that would remain

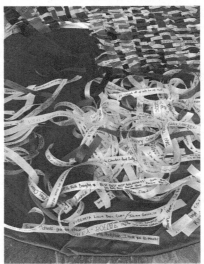

Pamela Nelson, *River of Time*, 2021. Photos by Cindy Ingram

unanswered, understanding that I have all the answers I need as I am today. I also didn't want to make it about me because I've spent my life making his pain about me. And while I don't have forgiveness, I now have compassion for his side of the story. I wrote simply, "I see you now."

That's what we all want, don't we?

To be seen. To be really seen.

Beneath the mask—inside of the mask

with all its stitched-up, fragile places.

It's one of the most fundamental human needs.

Seen and loved for all we truly are.

When I was ten crying in my room, I needed someone to say, "There there, Cindy. I see you. I'm here." Through my healing, I met that little girl and comforted her. I wrote her letters. I visualized parenting her and hugging her. It's twenty years too late for me to say that to my dad, but by writing it to him, I also wrote it to my ten-year-old self.

We're okay now.

We're together now in the everythingness of the universe.

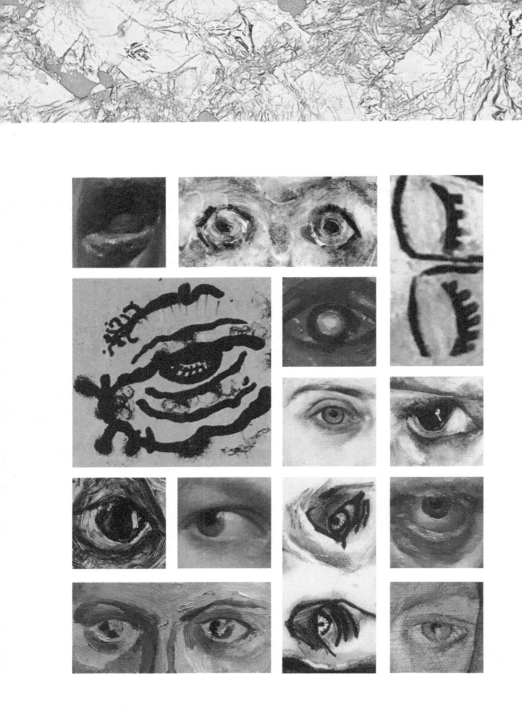

Vienna 1900

*Through the eyes of art,
I relish in the light of
shared humanity.*

It's been a long journey for me to be able to say things confidently like universe, energy, and even God. I was raised a Catholic, and I was a fervent one for a while. I immersed myself in the youth group at my church throughout middle and high school and even taught Sunday school to preschoolers. It was a home and a place where I felt safe, accepted, and loved. My friends at church were some of my best friends. I still fondly remember the donuts and Tang in the gym after church each Sunday, the lock-ins and the dances (made complete with the "Cotton-Eyed Joe" and the Macarena), us singing "LIFE IS A HIGHWAY AND I WANT TO RIDE IT ALL NIGHT LONG" (Cochrane, 1991) at the top of our lungs as we ran around acting silly and just enjoying being together. So many of my pivotal memories happened in that church gym, even my first slow dance to "On Bended Knee" by Boyz II Men. (What's Arthur Hernandez doing now? He was so fine.) I have nothing but love for that church, that building, Monsignor Tash (RIP), and those people I spent so much time with.

As a child and then a teen, I accepted Catholic doctrine as truth. That's what you do when you are a child—especially when the people telling you these things are the trusted people in your life. If you know any Catholics, though, you know that most kids born into the religion don't know nearly as much about Catholicism as those who converted later in life. As a child, you learn the basics, like an appetizer, and everything seems palatable. Later, they bring in the main entree—let's call it liver and onions—or purgatory, limbo, and transubstantiation.

I accepted the basics and went through the motions even as the entree was being prepared. I actually loved going to Mass—it was never a chore. I loved being in community, sitting next to my Papa, who would conspiratorially slip me Werther's Originals® "to hold me over until lunch," and resting my head on my mom's shoulder, enjoying the closeness that seemed sacred to me. I particularly loved the music—hearing all the voices together and feeling less alone. Listening to and singing the music in church is the closest I got to a "religious" experience, to that feeling of divine, of sublime. Only the arts could ever produce a feeling of the divine in my heart and soul. To me, the holy was intertwined with people engaging in art together, the swell of emotion in the score, and the power of the lyrics. Art transcends the music and the people into feeling and meaning.

With all that divine I felt in the music at church, I assumed it was God, so I prayed to Him like I was taught. I prayed a lot, mostly in tears, begging and pleading for God to bring back my dad. I never felt the connection in my prayers like in the music at church. I wondered if those prayers were making it to anyone's ears. But I needed someone to listen; that was the best I could do.

When I started my confirmation classes at sixteen—this is when you receive that main entree—I officially learned all of the rest of the "story" they sugar-coated in the years prior. At the end of those classes, you are supposed to confirm your decision to be Catholic, and that's when things started to get confusing. As creative as I am, I am also nothing if not logical. I test everything through my own internal system of logic. If I can't understand something, I can't agree to it. I can't believe it. And when they introduced purgatory after a childhood of the afterlife consisting of heaven and hell, they lost me. I remember exactly where I was sitting when I first had this feeling. Wait…what? Logic test failed. I was all about the music and community, but they lost me with purgatory. That's the extra level of the afterlife that broke the camel's back. One afterlife option too many (this was before I even learned about limbo, don't get me started on limbo). Nope.

So over the next few years, I slowly put down my Catholic faith. When I moved away to college, I didn't attend Mass. I did get married in my childhood church—for nostalgia and that sense of home more than anything. It was sad for me though. I loved my experience in church, and I wished I could believe what they believed. I see the comfort it gives people, and I longed for that. I eventually took a temporary-ish turn to atheism because it was the only thing that truly made sense to me. I've always been a big fan of science—especially space, paleontology, and genetics. Creating my belief system, or lack thereof, with science as the primary pillar made sense.

But as time passed, I realized that there was something I believed that didn't fit clearly with atheism either. The moment I dramatically connect with a work of art, until more recently, always stumped me. It felt bigger than just being a human on a rock flying through space who would one day die and become earth. My existence as a person felt more significant than that. I felt bigger than that. And I could see that each person I held dear—and even strangers—was bigger than just what was in their bodies.

How do you explain my deep intuition? How do you explain the spark that happens between two people? Between a person and art? Between a person and the expansiveness of the universe. Yes, science has theories on all of that. Our bodies' wisdom gets more and more understandable to science as time passes, but when I emotionally react to a work of art, I am connected with something bigger than myself. For a moment, I am connected to that artist, another person from another time and another place. I feel I am not alone in the world; I understand my place. It provides me just what religion provides people, without the stories I don't believe, the extra layers of the afterlife, and the one all-powerful God ruling it all. With art, I see that someone made something from their heart, which has now entered my own. It's a pure, sweet, blissful, and sublime experience.

It's more than atheism, but it's not religion. It's spiritual but not dogmatic. It's personal. When I try to describe my spirituality, I usually say that I believe in the power of the human spirit. I believe in the magic we carry. I believe that God (whatever God is) is seen in the connections between people, in my mind, in my heart, and in my soul, all at the same time.

John Koenig, the creator of the *Dictionary of Obscure Sorrows*, invented the word *sonder*, which seems to describe this experience for me. *Sonder* is

"the realization that each random passerby is living a life as vivid and complex as your own—populated with their own ambitions, friends, routines, worries and inherited craziness—an epic story that continues invisibly around you like an anthill sprawling deep underground, with elaborate passageways to thousands of other lives that you'll never know existed, in which you might appear only once, as an extra sipping coffee in the background, as a blur of traffic passing on the highway, as a lighted window at dusk."

Sometimes I get sad when I realize I will never fully understand or know another person as well as I would want to (especially my children). When I connect spiritually with the art someone made, I briefly connect with the infinity of our existence on this planet. There is the realization that I am intimately connecting with another person, that many others before and after me will connect with the same thing, and that it all originated in the mind, body, and spirit of a single person expressing their truth. Suddenly, my inner world and the outer world of humanity feel simultaneously connected and expansive.

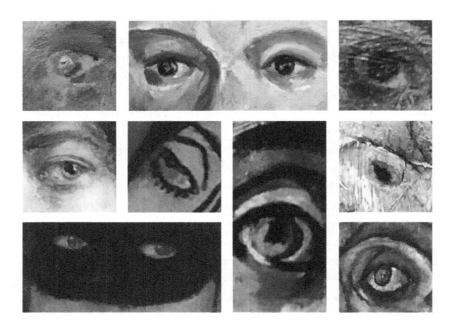

Sonder

I see you
as you cross the street
a stranger in another life
another body
another mind

We catch eyes
and your full existence
floods into my field

I see

The fullness of me is the fullness of you
The complexity of me is the complexity of you.
The humanity of me is the humanity of you
The divinity of me is the divinity of you

Our atoms were once swirling together in the universe
part of us dinosaurs munching on shoots and leaves
part of us stars and planets and rocks hurtling through space
part of us common ancestors inching forward
towards
consciousness

We were once nothing but atoms with no awareness
of who or what we were
and what we were a part

Now we are two separate bodies
two separate minds
living in two separate universes
just footsteps from each other

And as you cross the street
our eyes meet
a moment of recognition
we were once one
a moment of recognition
maybe we still are

Never has this experience of *sonder* come to me so intently as when I visited the *Vienna 1900* exhibit at the Leopold Museum in Vienna, Austria, in the summer of 2019. The exhibit showed the birth of Modern art, primarily portraits that became more abstract and expressive as the exhibition went on. As I went from room to room, I started to fixate on the eyes of each of the portraits. Each portrait became more than just an artwork, but an experience of another person, another soul, and also somehow a part of me. I felt like I understood my place on this planet in a way I never had before. I started to photograph close-up shots of the eyes and ended up making a video of all of these shots from the exhibit, watching the eyes morph from realistic to expressive as the video continued, mimicking my emotions as I went through—the more eyes I connected with, the more emotional I became.

" He's aware of [her] beside him.
Her molecules are mixing with his;
he's not just himself; he's made up
of her too. Which means he's composed
of everyone he's ever touched,
everyone he's ever shaken hands with,
hugged, or high-fived. That means
he has molecules inside him
from his parents and. . .everyone else. "

— Ann Napolitano in *Dear Edward*

My connection to art is a connection with my humanity and the humanity of others. In us all are worlds of our own creations. We are the same but also different, and my spirituality now honors the divinity in each of us. Whenever I fully pursue the question of who, where, or what god is, I always come back to I am god. But also, so are you.

I Am God

Every night as a child
I prayed to God as I was taught.
Every night
alone, I begged.
Bring back my dad.

Searching,
with my prayers and my longing,
desperate
to be seen,
to be heard.
I found no solace.
I found no mercy.

Grasping
into the void,
I found nothing.
No wrathful, punishing God
Nor a merciful one

I did not feel His presence
Let alone His solace,
His mercy,
His love.

In those dark nights
left by my father
and my God,
there was only me.

I was not enough,
but I was all I had.

What I now know:
God was indeed with me
Because I was there

God is
not an all powerful being
giving and taking away

God is
Expansiveness
Awe
Connection

God is
knowing
the past, present, and future
are all here
now.

To that pleading child,
I send God

God's mercy
God's compassion
God's love

And while she didn't feel it then
She can feel it
now
She is in me, and
I am God.

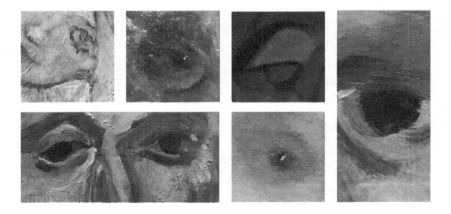

Image Credits for this Chapter (in order of appearance):
All images photographed by Cindy Ingram, July 2019.

Alfred Hrdlicka, *Portrait Oskar Kokoschka II (detail)*, 1964

Egon Schiele, *Mother and child (detail)*, 1912

Rudolf Kalvach, *Holy family (detail)*, 1907-08

Oscar Kokoschka, *Poster 'The Storm' (detail)*, 1910

Arnold Schönberg, *Gaze (Karl Kraus) (detail)*, 1910

Anton Romako, *Portrait of Isabella Reisser (detail)*, 1885

Egon Schiele, *Mourning woman (detail)*, 1912

Egon Schiele, *Self-portrait with raised bare shoulder (detail)*, 1912

Gustav Klimt, *Head study of a girl from Haná (detail)*, 1883

Oskar Kokoschka, *Pietà. Poster for his play 'Murderer, Hope of Women' at the Internationale Kunstschau, Vienna (detail)*, 1909

Albert Birkle, *Man with fur cap (My brother the animal) (detail)*, 1923

Arnold Schönberg, *Emil Hertzka (detail)*, c. 1910

Egon Schiele, *Portrait of Poldi Lodzinsky (detail)*, 1910

Arnold Schönberg, *Christ (detail)*, c. 1910

Arnold Schönberg, *Mathilde Schönberg (detail)*, c. 1910

Egon Schiele, *Lovers (unfinished) (detail)*, 1918

Franz von Lenbach, *Franziska von Wertheimstein (detail)*, c. 1870

Rudolf Kalvach, *Holy family (detail)*, 1907-08

Oskar Kokoschka, *Self-portrait at the easel (detail)*, 1922

Egon Schiele, *Mother with Two Children II (detail)*, 1915

Max Kurzweil, *Female Nude with Mask Before the Mirror (detail)*, 1907

Egon Schiele, *Transfiguration (The blind II) (detail)*, 1915

Gustav Klimt, *Death and life (detail)*, 1915

Gustav Klimt, *The blind man (detail)*, c. 1896

Egon Schiele, *Seated nude (Self-portrait) (detail)*, c. 1910

Arnold Schönberg, *Gustav Mahler (detail)*, 1910

Arnold Schönberg, *Alexander Zemlinksy (detail)*, 1910

Gustav Klimt, *Lady with hat on a red background (detail)*, 1907-08

Brooke Shaden, *Let Loose the Curious Being*, 2015
Image courtesy of the artist

"Light! give me light!" was the wordless cry of my soul,

Let Loose
the Curious Being

Holding myself back,
true connection can't be forged.
Let loose the real me.

Sometimes when you are in the midst of healing—doing all the work, utilizing all the supports available—there are still areas that lurk in the shadows of every room, a constant, unspoken reminder that you still have more to do. It's unrelenting, but in a nondescript way, a seed underneath the soil that you can feel growing but don't want to acknowledge. My marriage was that for me, and I wouldn't let any coaches, healers, or even myself near it. I felt like a new person, but something was wrong at home, and I wasn't ready to talk about it. I couldn't admit it to myself or anyone. I actively did all I could to pretend these feelings of disconnection weren't percolating in the back of my mind. Doubt, uncertainty, and confusion were constant. I loved my husband, but I wondered: amid all this healing, were we now too different? Were we still "right" for each other?

My husband is steady, emotionally stable. He's nonjudgmental and has never seemed to care about societal expectations. For example, I used to be so confused when we were never invited to the yearly family reunions on his side of the family. It turns out we were invited, but he just never told me. He didn't want to go, so he said no and moved on, not even thinking to mention it to me. No hemming and hawing about what the family would think or whether or not our absence would upset anyone, as I would have done. Anytime I would get in my head worrying about how I appear to others or wondering if I was hurting someone's feelings, he would just look at me confused and shrug. For someone so wrapped up in how she appears to others, it felt amazing to be with someone who just didn't seem to have that trait at all. I wanted to jump into his brain and feel that freedom, not to be wrapped up in other people and just be 100 percent my own. I knew I could be myself around him, unmasked with my idiosyncrasies, neuroses, and sensitivities on full display. He's not social at all, so he didn't force my social anxiety into uncomfortable situations. I have always known he loved me, and he tells me often. I always trusted that. He is trustworthy, loyal, consistent, and logical—the complete opposite of my emotional, spontaneous, ambitious, and neurotic chaos. The yang to my yin. And ultimately, he is so kind and warm—a comfort, a balm to my wounds.

> **She's the sea; she needs a rock to crash against.**
> — Catriona Silvey in *Meet Me in Another Life*

I had a lot of baggage coming into our relationship (feelings of abandonment and emotional distance were constant), and he was my haven. Looking back at my young adult self, I can see why he became my anchor. I firmly believed I could not be loved, yet he loved me. I didn't have relationships I could trust, and he provided the steadiness of that emotional support I needed. I chose someone who I knew I could trust and who loved me unconditionally, neuroses and sensitivities and all. I felt safe and secure in that love. I needed to be held in that way. We started dating the summer after graduating high school, and we married a year after I graduated from college. As we grew up, we worked to stabilize our finances (we were so broke for so long), and then we had kids. I healed through all of it, inherently knowing I was preparing for something big in my life. (I was preparing to write this book, hello.) I was preparing to soar, but he wasn't. And as I prepared to let my creativity loose, he longed for the steady stability we had cultivated over the years.

I didn't know he didn't like to travel because we were too broke to travel. I didn't know he didn't want to move to all the places because we didn't have that option. When I started to spread my wings, he began to pull his back in. Whereas I used him as a haven from which to jump off the cliff into the life I wanted, he had no interest in cliff jumping and wanted to anchor himself to the foundation we had built. His anxiety began as mine dissipated.

As I went out into the world, it was initially a deliberate choice to—in a way—turn against my husband and where he was comfortable. In 2014, when I started my business and started traveling more, I decided I would do what I wanted, whether he wanted that or not. If he didn't want to travel, I would go alone. If he didn't desire a social life, I would build one without him. I couldn't stay small and hold back from what I wanted.

But I wasn't who he married at the young age of twenty-three. I had released so much from the identity that I had gripped so tightly for so long, and I was becoming more and more myself every day—learning who I was without shame. Recalling Erik Johansson's *Grow with Progress*, I had made it to the top of those stairs growing with each and every step. I finally knew what it was like to be 100 percent my own, but now my stable anchor of marriage felt more like a disconnected rope dangling in the water. I wasn't willing to take a compassionate, curious look because I didn't want to admit that something was broken because I didn't want to hurt him or my girls. I loved that they had the loving, caring, and present dad I lacked in my bio-dad, and I couldn't fathom that I could be the cause of blowing up their lives. I was worried that my husband and I had become too different and we wanted two different things in life. I wasn't sure I was who he needed, and I wasn't sure he could give me what I needed. There was this little squirming thought in the back of my mind: is this still enough?

❋ ❋ ❋

So yes, I was at the top of the cliffs looking into the future, but unlike the protagonist in this chapter's artwork, *Let Loose the Curious Being* by Brooke Shaden, I was still bound at my wrists, attached, and wanting to cut the ropes free. And these ropes aren't a metaphor for my husband. He wasn't holding me back. I was holding myself back with this fear of truly expressing how I felt. I spent a large part of my life stuffing down my feelings, thinking that if I showed people the real feelings inside of me, they would leave me. I would be abandoned and alone. The ropes for me were a manifestation of my lack of trust that other people can love me and will stay and fight for me. I bound myself with those ropes, but I desperately wanted to cut them loose. In this photograph, a woman confidently thrusts herself off a red rocky canyon into an unknown space backed by a cloudy, tumultuous gold and black sky. Released from her bind, cut ropes trail from her wrists. Pushing her chest and heart forward with her eyes closed and her chin up, she doesn't know what will happen after her jump, but she fully trusts herself. She is leaping.

With everything I learned while swimming to avoid "Bruce," you'd think I would have learned not to avoid facing the hard things in my life. Interestingly, the lessons we need to learn are ones we must meet repeatedly, as much as we might not like it. Every time facing these lessons gets easier, but mastery is elusive. Self-trust, conquering shame, feeling my feelings, expressing those feelings, and body acceptance are lessons I know I will have to continue to learn again and again and again for the rest of my life. Each time I get a little stronger in my resolve. It gets easier—the emotions more familiar and the way through more apparent—but life will be a place of learning no matter what.

* * *

Before this moment of breaking the ropes and leaning into my future, that tumultuous sky mimicked my internal environment around my husband. What I know about a turbulent sky after all the years of living in Texas is that the most dangerous storms happen when the sky becomes eerie, uncertain, and unfamiliar. And that was how I felt inside, uncertain, off-balance, stuck—bound and trapped in my idea of a relationship I didn't recognize anymore. I was scared—not really of him but of my feelings about him. I would feel nervous anticipation when I heard his office chair creak, meaning he was getting up and coming through whatever room I was in. I would resent him not spending time with my family when they visited or engaging with our family friends when we would all get together. I would resent being the default parent, the one who had to keep track of all the things—knowing when kids needed new socks or shoes, keeping track of school and extracurricular schedules, paying all the bills, and managing the emotional and thinking burden of running a family. But at the time I could see all the good too. How he was a fully engaged dad. How he could easily weave in and out of caring for the children without me having to write an owner's manual. How much we all felt his fierce love, protection, and devotion.

So I was in avoidance again, and this time the avoidance came when a lot of other shit was going down. In the Fall of 2021, I was going through a rough patch—midway through a yearlong bout of anxiety and depression. I had just laid off two of my beloved employees and was devastated and wracked with guilt. I was sad for my business to lose them, but more sorry to have disappointed them and let them down. The anxiety from that decision stayed in my body even though I knew it was the right (and only) decision for the future of my business, my family, and even me.

At the same time, I was in turmoil about things in my personal life. As they tend to do, mental health issues made everything more challenging. I felt very stuck in the overwhelm of the day-to-day family life that had been ramping up again after the Covid lockdowns. Carpool text threads, dog surgery and aftercare, kids' sports games and theater rehearsals, Girl Scout meetings, cooking, cleaning. All the things felt too hard and too much. It felt so overwhelming just to do basic care tasks for myself and family. I tend to take too much ownership over everything because appearing needy could also lead to someone leaving me, so I subconsciously don't ask for help when I need it. I felt less joy and connection; all I wanted to do was burrow into my cocoon of pillows and blankets and play video games or watch tv. A big part of me yearned for the simplicity of March and April 2020—when the world stopped, and I took a big deep breath as responsibilities halted and self-care and relaxation became paramount. I felt like I was drowning in all areas of my life and didn't know how to save myself.

I started working with Yola Mehmeti, a highly-intuitive Theta healer who can see right through me to the core of who I am. She's the most intuitive person I ever met, so my strategy of not letting any coach or therapist talk with me about my marriage flat out didn't work on her. During one session, she commented that my overwhelm at home wouldn't be so dramatic if I wasn't dancing around the doubts in the back of my mind about my husband (we had not once talked about any of these doubts, tight-lipped as I was). She noted that to her, my overwhelm felt like it was about something deeper.

Begrudgingly I knew she was right, and I had to do something about these feelings. I also knew that, at last, I was ready to face whatever came my way with my new emotional intelligence and self-trust. I started to allow myself to go there—to think about the thing I had been pushing down, to feel the feelings, to let breathe whatever was lurking beneath the surface, and then give myself the strength to face it. There was so much fear about those feelings I had stuffed down. Facing them meant acknowledging that what I might find might also lead me to an answer I wasn't ready or willing to accept. Facing my feelings meant that I could end up with a devastating outcome. But I also knew that if I dealt with this lurking disconnection, I could find a place where we were more aligned, and I wouldn't have this burden of fear poisoning the back of my brain as I moved through my days. But to become unstuck and break those ropes I had tied to my wrists, I needed to embrace the uncertainty, knowing that things could fall apart, but that things falling apart was better than walking around overwhelmed with doubt and resentment.

Around the same time as Yola's observation, my close friend's daughter was diagnosed autistic, and my friend and her daughter educated us on what this meant for them, and we spent time seeing this delightful girl I had known for years through this new lens. As my friend would mention things about her daughter's personality that can now be attributed to autism, some bells were starting to ping in my head. Hmm. Eric does that. Hmm. Eric is that way too. Hmm.

✳ ✳ ✳

Just as I had been able to look at my past self and bio-dad with a new compassionate curiosity, I turned that gaze onto my husband. I saw his ability to pull a movie quote out of thin air, any movie quote, a quote from a movie he saw once in 1997. I saw his ability to relate any life situation to a plot line in *Star Trek DS9*. I saw how he kept his office lights off or down so low that I could not see anything if I went in. I saw how when my family would visit, he wouldn't spend as much time with us as I wanted him to. I saw how he would shut down in stressful situations like travel. I saw how he seemed a little more robotic in social situations, putting on a different personality that didn't make sense with who I knew at home. I saw his commitment to consistency and stability. I saw why my spontaneous, chaotic, entrepreneurial lifestyle directly opposed his nature. I saw his constant need to drum on things, whistle, and mimic little noises (all of which drove me completely batty). And his ability to not care what other people think that I mentioned earlier? There might be a reason for all of these things. He didn't seem to care about how society thinks he should be. I saw how even though my anxieties caused me to be hyper-aware of most people's emotions, I never could read his. They never made sense to me. Sometimes I'd be convinced he was experiencing some deep emotional pain from the look on his face, and then he'd start giggling about something from Reddit or get up and make a peanut butter and jelly sandwich.

Holy mother of Hufflepuff, how did we not see it? HOW DID WE NOT SEE IT? His autism was so obvious that my mind was completely blown. Suddenly with this realization, the last twenty years of my relationship with this person made complete sense. How did we not see it? He pursued the path of an official diagnosis which he (and my two daughters) subsequently received.

Once I noticed these patterns in his behavior and seeing our relationship through this new lens, I started reading about relationships between autistic people and their partners, and so much became clear. I finally felt like I had some words to describe the off-ness of our relationship. I have learned that there can be a disconnect when the spouse of an autistic partner expects to get their emotional needs met in a certain way by their partner. In our interactions, I can see how I had put unrealistic expectations on him and how he unknowingly shut me out. A common characteristic of autism is alexithymia, not being able to identify one's own emotionss, so it made complete sense that I couldn't read his emotions as he couldn't often read his own. Another trait of autism is struggling with reciprocal social interaction and communication, so I often misinterpreted his actions and motives.

And through this lens, I started to see what was really happening in our relationship. I realized that the emotional deprivation I felt from my husband was familiar to what I experienced with my family growing up where my emotions were often not understood or I felt as if my emotions were an inconvenience to others. For instance, when I would try to share my feelings with my husband, he would unknowingly shut me down, and over time this conditioned me not to say anything at all. That created a slow deterioration of our relationship and our ability to communicate. Just like in high school when I wanted to find my bio-dad and had to confront my sister about my pain, I felt that same fear of opening up, of appearing weak, and of being shut out emotionally. When I wanted to say something important about how I felt to my husband, I would spend hours in fear—actual fear—before I could get the courage to say what I wanted to say. I was afraid I would hurt his feelings and there's nothing worse than being the cause of someone else's pain. It also felt unsafe because he wouldn't say anything, dismiss it as unimportant, or turn it back on me. I often didn't feel heard or understood, making me feel confused and stupid and like I was speaking another language. Feeling wounded, I was defensive and raw from years of mismatched communication, but holding it together so as to make sure everyone else in my family felt happy and safe. I chose to keep everyone safe by keeping myself quiet because I thought it was necessary; that was how I had survived.

Only in the last few years did I realize that having conversations is something I am actually good at, and I now talk to people for a living with my podcast and *Art Connection Circle*. For so long before this realization, and because of my husband's autism, my introversion, and my family's way of communicating, I felt like an idiot anytime I tried to speak. I thought I wasn't interesting, that I didn't have important things to say, that I was too easily misunderstood, that I was awkward, or that I was boring. I was so scared of being misunderstood and being left behind by the people I loved most. It turns out all those things I was scared of were not true. Even so, I felt them, and healing from those wounds took a lot of time.

✳ ✳ ✳

So there I was, like I imagine the woman in *Let Loose the Curious Being* would be in the minutes before her leap, in a tumultuous, emotional internal state—a yellow, cloudy, thunderous sky as her companion—chaos and a rift within her. It was a moment of reckoning. I had never allowed myself to examine the ropes that bound my wrists because sometimes it is easier to stay stuck than to face the truth. Sometimes it is easier to remain powerless and voiceless rather than rock the boat. But if I wanted to experience something like freedom, if I wanted to practice and stand strong in all the work I had done for myself on self-trust, on self-acceptance, on emotional literacy, on boundaries, of fighting for myself, of learning who I am and that I am valuable and unbroken, I had to start taking the steps I was still scared to take. Not up a staircase to a clear destination like in *Grow with Progress*, but off the cliff to who knows where. At the same time, I knew that jumping into the future is claiming what I want, need, and deserve out of life.

And so, bound and uncomfortable on the red rocks with the wind uneasily shaking my footing, I allowed myself to consider the options to free myself from this situation—the situation not being the marriage but the situation of doubting, of resenting, of fear, of wonder, of being stuck, of disconnection. The questions pin-balled in my mind:

How will I be able to face this conversation?

How can I explain how I feel without breaking my husband's heart?

How can I love him without being sure we are right for each other?

Can he give me what I need, and if not, will he ever be able to, knowing what we know now?

Can I give him what he needs?

How would I feel if he felt the same way?

For the first time, I finally allowed myself to really think about the answers to these questions. I realized that until now, I had not allowed myself to fully express how I felt. I had merely been tip-toeing around my feelings, afraid to look at them in the face. So, in this moment of exploring these questions and the answers that came up for me, I allowed myself a choice, and once I knew I had a choice, my wrists were released from the ropes that bound them. I had my power back, and I knew what I had to do.

> **"** I feel lighter, relieved of a burden.
> Sharing difficult truths might come
> with a cost—the need to face them—
> but there's also a reward: freedom.
> The truth releases us from shame. **"**
> — Lori Gottlieb in *Maybe You Should Talk to Someone*

✳ ✳ ✳

One of the books I read when we discovered my husband might be autistic recommended writing him a letter. A letter would allow me to fully say all I wanted to say without fear of being misunderstood or getting stifled by emotion. It would give his brain what he needs too—clarity of communication and plenty of processing time, not being put on the spot with information or coming to snap judgments.

So I poured my heart into a four-page letter—some of those words even made their way into this chapter. I told him how exciting his autism diagnosis is and how his knowing himself and me knowing him better makes everything in our relationship so much more clear. But I also told him about my emotions, about how I felt like I was taking on some of his traits throughout the years, questioning myself. I told him about my experience of feeling shut down by his lack of social reciprocity and how familiar it was to being shut down as a child. But the ultimate point of the letter was a call out for connection, telling him how I felt profoundly lonely and disconnected in our relationship. And I didn't know what to do about it, especially with the new knowledge that our brains are fundamentally wired differently, but that the first step was to admit it and start the conversation.

I leapt like the figure in Shaden's photograph. Head up, shoulders back, eyes closed, chin and heart forward. Her hands clench on her now-broken restraints, and she is leaning into what's next. She's making that fall forward intentionally, with resolve. She's confident that she can handle whatever happens next. It may be easy or it may be hard, but she knows she has the skills and resilience and heart and emotional literacy and tools and all the things to handle whatever she faces next. The expression on her face is not afraid and not excited—whether or not she is feeling any of that—not anything but calm resolve, but the slight clench of her jaw shows she is ready.

✳ ✳ ✳

Handing that letter I wrote to my husband was a scary thing. I wasn't used to allowing my opinions to be heard, sharing and owning my feelings, and claiming what I want and deserve in this life. That was entirely too vulnerable and too risky. In some regards, this was one of the last places I was holding myself back. I let myself out—I let myself loose—with that letter. I freed myself from one of the last places where I was holding myself down. And it was one of the best things I have ever done. In the letter, I invited my husband to take his time processing it, but he rushed to me after reading it. He opened himself up with love and curiosity. As he had always done in our marriage, he heard my feelings and didn't judge them. He believed me. He allowed me to feel and express what I felt. I saw why I chose him and remembered why he was so good for me. We spent hours and days in conversation, challenging ourselves to be honest and vulnerable, not be afraid of each other, and share our hearts and truths.

I knew this letter could either pull us apart or bring us together, and I was so grateful that what happened was a reaffirmation of why we were together. When I wrote this letter, we had been together for twenty-two years and married for eighteen of those years. My husband has been with me for all of my growth, and we have been together longer than we have been apart. I was a scared, anxious, and insecure person when we met. He was a comfort to me then, even if I didn't understand why he loved me, and through my growth I worried that I had become just too different. In our conversations after this letter, we met each other again and got reacquainted as now forty-year-olds—releasing those eighteen-year-old versions of ourselves and stepping into what is next.

What I learned through this process was profound. I learned that to move forward is to express myself without fear (or more like feel the fear and do it anyway). I learned that years of shutting out myself, locking in and zipping up all those feelings squashed so much of the artist and writer in me, of my natural state. In the months after the letter, I uncovered my own neurodiversity, adding new layers of understanding and compassion for who I am. I realized that all along, I felt like an alien when I entered any room because I really am an alien, and that is actually the best thing. When I let loose my own curious being—when I communicate who I am fearlessly, and when I allow myself to be unapologetically me, I can make magic happen.

I believe that Art contains the answers and provides a safe haven, a place where I can be fully me. It reminds me over and over, "Wholeness is…"

Shahzia Sikander, *Mary Magdalene*, 2009. Ink, opaque watercolor, and watercolor on clay-coated paper. 16.5 x 12 inches. Created for Met Opera Exhibit "Something About Mary." Image courtesy of the artist.

PART THREE

Becoming Art

Wholeness is embracing life,
its mess and chaos.
Accepting that you contain multitudes
of thoughts, experiences,
good, bad, and in between.

Wholeness is compassionate,
unashamed curiosity
towards your humanity and
who you are becoming.

Wholeness is seeing a path forward and
finding peace in the journey.

Wholeness is a process
not a destination.

You are alive here in the embrace of Art.

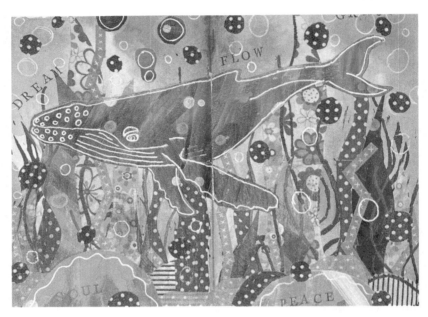

Cindy Ingram, *Whale*, 2022

Practicing Art

Laying down my wounds,
I lean into the process.
Becoming, artist.

Cindy Ingram, *Strange and Sweet World*, 2023

Everything I have gone through, every lesson I have learned, every tear
I have shed, every success, every setback have all kept me moving. I once

thought I was moving towards a fixed place, a goal of being valuable, worthy, and successful. But somewhere along the way, I realized the goal was no longer a destination but a process of wholeness. And it isn't an external shift; it's a shift inward. For the first time in my life, I truly recognize that the answers to my questions cannot be found anywhere else other than inside of me. And I can see who I am clearly.

I've been there all along, but hiding—under protective armor, under layers of shame, under masks of "put-together-ness." But that whisper that comes from the art, that's the whisper of me on the inside. When Picasso's *Girl Before a Mirror* zapped me out of the Ph.D. application process, when the second Frida sent her compassion to my hurting inner child, and when a poem about Aleah Chapin's *The Opening* flooded into my mind during a sound bath at the yoga studio, all of these moments from this book, and even moments that didn't make this story, led me back to myself. Cutting through all the noise, I can hear myself now. I am the art, and the art is me.

Cindy Ingram, *I Am Moana*, 2023. Quotation from *I am Moana (Song of the Ancestors)*

It was a lightning strike of a moment in December 2021. I was meditating on what was next. Pondering the question, how do I show people the power of art? How do I show them what art can do for them? And I was not expecting the answer that rang long and clear. "Through your art." MY ART?!? Hell no. I'm listening now, yeah, but at the time, I was not ready for THAT. My immediate reaction was surprise at the sheer clarity of that message, followed by outright denial. Nooooooo, I thought, I can't possibly do that. Even though I've spent most of my life working and teaching with works of art and connecting deeply with art that others have made, I've kept making my own art at a safe arms-length away. Of course, I would make examples for my classroom, paint with my kids, make the posters for the pep rally and things at school, but my own art just for me? I hadn't done that in a good twenty years. My degree is in art history, I would say. That's my real passion. And it was and still is; looking at art is my fuel, and that will not change. But I know both can be true—I can be an artist and still feel deeply about the art others have made.

Somewhere along the way, after being the little kid who couldn't stop drawing and creating, a kid who wanted to be a Disney® animator AND write the score for the production (I came out of the womb ambitious apparently), I became committed to the story that I wasn't creative or talented enough and that I didn't have enough good ideas to truly be an "artist." Although I was usually a star student in all of my art classes growing up, there were also one or two students who had a natural talent that I just didn't have. I could capture the right proportions for a drawing, but they could model and shade it to look realistic. I could create a bold composition, but they could create a masterpiece. It sunk in during my Drawing I class in college when my professor gave me a B after exclaiming in my end-of-course critique that I was the hardest-working, most committed student. I wanted to be as good as those naturally talented students, but I never felt I could keep up.

> **❝** Every child is an artist. The problem is how to remain an artist once we grow up. **❞**
> —Pablo Picasso

Anytime I tried to start making art again over the years, I would be thwarted by overwhelm, sky-high expectations, and perfectionism. One of the reasons I didn't create visual art for so long in my life was that I was very rigid in my view of what it meant to make art and to be an artist. I thought I had to have an idea first, and then my job was to create the thing I saw in my head. Despite all of my knowledge to the contrary, I somehow believed that the art had to be planned and thought through first, and then and only then do you make the piece. My art and art history professors continually drilled into my psyche the "artist as genius" trope throughout my education. I was no genius. I was a mess.

Of course, that's not how it must be—rigid, pre-planned, and perfect. With ADHD, that's not how I do anything in life. When I travel to a new place, I just show up and start exploring. I don't read guidebooks. When cooking, I start with what I have on hand, maybe referencing a recipe or two for the temperature and timing so that I don't poison anybody. I never make the same thing the same way twice, much to the chagrin of the "sameness" preferences of my autistic husband and children. But my life has always been more spontaneous, more expressive. Hell, I even wrote almost a whole entirely different book before this version came through; it formed and reformed itself many times through the process of me showing up daily for my writing practice. The process showed me what was true, not my brain in a pre-planning, perfectionistic state.

Why did I think my art had to be anything less than an extension of me and how I naturally move through this life? Of course, I logically know that each artist has their own process and their own way of creating, that art is an extension of the artist, and that art comes from a primal soulful–human–place within. But somewhere along the way, I internalized that my way was wrong. I had to do it another way, and if I didn't do it that way, I shouldn't do it at all.

※ ※ ※

Something changed at the end of 2021, though. I had a zap of knowing that it was time for me to make art again. I had to stop avoiding it. I was meant to make art, and every day of me ignoring the call to make art was me denying my true self, denying the authentic me I had worked so hard to rediscover.

I'd like to say that when I got the download to make art, I immediately sprung into action. And I did for a minute; I made a painting for Madalyn as a gift to celebrate some brutal but badass moves she made in her life, but a good eight months stood between the creation of that painting to when I started to make art regularly.

I first used logistical considerations as my primary excuse. My office is small, and with the computer and work stuff, there's not a lot of room to make art. I tried working with watercolor since that was easy to do in a small space, but watercolor isn't a medium I particularly enjoy as it is way too hard to be spontaneous when you have to pre-plan where you want to leave white. And then my ADHD can't handle the executive function needed to move art supplies in and out of the kitchen when I want to create, so that didn't work either. So I set out to create an art space for me and my children in our house.

Months later, the space was complete, with desks and storage and all the supplies handy. It's a beautiful space, but did I use it once completed? Nope. I finally had to dig deep and figure out my blocks around making art. Namely, I realized my perfectionism was my biggest block. If I didn't know for sure that what I would make would be "good," then I wouldn't even start doing it.

I've always loved looking at people's art journal spreads online, so I started to play with the idea of what would happen if I allowed myself to make marks and glue stuff down into an art journal. What if I let it happen without having an idea or a plan? What if I just let myself play? Then if it wasn't "good," it didn't matter. I could just flip the page. This could work.

At age eighty-four, Kurt Vonnegut (2006) replied to a group of high school students who wrote him a letter and told them to write a poem, not share it with anyone, tear it into pieces, and throw it away in multiple trash cans. Then he said, "You will find that you have already been gloriously rewarded for your poem. You have experienced becoming, learned a lot more about what's inside you, and you have made your soul grow." That's what I was hoping for with the art journal.

Cindy Ingram, *Magic Woman*, 2023. Woman collaged from *The Magic Dreidels: A Hannukkah Story* by Eric A. Kimmel illustrated by Katya Krenina

Space created? Check. Brain and emotions analyzed? Check and check. Type of art chosen? Check. Supplies purchased? Check. But still, no art was being made. I realized I needed to force myself into that art room to make art. I knew I wanted to and that I would love it once I started, but I needed to build some structure into my life. I needed to force that little snowball over the edge so that it could gain momentum and start to grow into a snow-head. As you may imagine, structure and I have never seen eye to eye. I can't follow plans or recipes; I can't stay organized. I love an all-consuming project that takes over my hyper-focus for days, but a long-term, regular practice? That's not something I've ever been particularly successful at…until…this book happened.

Midway through the creation of the art studio, I started in earnest to write this book. For a year or two, I worked on it here and there when I had bursts of inspiration. I took a class; I worked on an outline. I puttered around with it. But because it couldn't be perfect out the gate, because it wasn't something I could throw myself into and finish quickly, I couldn't get any movement forward. That was until I made the decision and the commitment to write the book. A year ago, from the writing of this book, I joined my writing group, *The Writing Practice*, led by Heather Doyle Fraser of the Compassionate Mind Collaborative, my publishing partner, development editor, and book coach. I had taken her *Compassionate Writer* course and knew she was the one who could lead me through this process.

I inherently knew that if I wanted this book to be written, I had to behave like someone who writes books. I had to show up every day. I had to write whether I felt like it or not. I had to face the challenging emotions that came up. I had to lay the bricks, chop the wood, and carry the water. Day by day by week by month, I had to show up. So I joined the Writing Practice with the commitment that I would attend every session, no matter what. This meant I scheduled all other meetings around writing practice. This meant I couldn't skip because I wanted to sleep in or skip because my family wanted to get ice cream. This daily choice and commitment to this project made all the difference for me. Over a year of attending the Writing Practice, I am forever changed.

Showing up for my daily writing has taught my brain, "I do this now." Because most of the writing practice is in the morning, when I wake up, my brain kicks in and starts to write, whether or not it was the plan for the day. And because my brain now knows I write every day, my subconscious is always looking for new input for the creative problems I am solving, and it sees connections constantly. After writing some chapters, I became convinced I was a witch. How the right thing would show up at the exact right time, how the things I was writing would show up in my life. Louis Pasteur said, "Chance favors the prepared mind," and I have absolutely found this to be true during this time.

Perhaps the most significant change in my commitment to my daily writing practice was the realization that the process is everything. At the end of my writing practice, I may not have "made progress" toward the things I have created, but the process of engaging with my creativity is progress, even if no words were written on the page. Before, writing had the same blocks as I had with art. It was something that had to be perfect. I had to have the perfect idea, and my job was to execute it perfectly the first time. To flow the words onto the page in already-beautiful prose as I feel a divine muse work magic through me. No. Well, sometimes. But mostly, no.

Sometimes I wrestle. Sometimes I cry. Sometimes it's therapy. Sometimes it's checking my email every five seconds or going to refill my coffee, trying to distract myself. Sometimes I write a thousand words in an hour; sometimes I delete a whole chapter, setting me back in word count but forward in clarity and cohesion. But in the end, all of it moves me forward slowly. It has been all about the process. And in the end, I will have a beautiful product I am proud of that you are reading now, but now I show up and do the work every day.

And life has always been all about the process—when I lived an ambitious life, when I was always working toward perfection and the next goal post, moving it further away with each success, and when I was striving for a moment of "you have arrived and you are no longer broken." My daily writing practice has shown me every day that there is no artist as genius—creating their perfect idea and implementing it to perfection. Artists and writers are humans with all the same feelings I have—the insecurities, the anxiety, and the fear, working daily on their process, moving forward slowly and with intention.

※ ※ ※

Back in the depths of my burnout, I had gotten to a point where I couldn't write. I outsourced it to my personal "writer as genius" on my team, Madalyn. The thought of writing even a few sentences sent me into shutdown, so it was a big moment when I realized I am a writer. It happened on my drive home from therapy, which I had to start again since this book was bringing up so many emotions. See, therapy is at nine am on Fridays, and writing practice is at ten, so I rush home to make it to writing practice because I do. not. skip. writing practice, even if I must show up a few minutes late. Pondering my therapy session and looking forward to writing practice, I suddenly realized, "I am a writer." I instantly started to cry. There is so much power and healing in that truth. And I know it must sound weird for someone whose book you have just nearly finished to proclaim she is a writer, but it was pro-found. And it still is. This realization gave me the courage to write and include poems in this book. I wrote many poems as a child, and when my editor suggested I consider poetry, I broke down because it felt like coming home to myself—remembering a part of myself that I had long forgotten.

Cindy Ingram, *Goldilocks*, 2022. Goldilocks and troll collaged from *The Ladybird Book of Fairy Tales*, retold by Rose Impey, Illustrated by John Dyke, Brian Price Thomas, Robert Lumley, Eric Winter, Harry Wingfield, and Martin Aitchison

" Practice any art...no matter how well or badly, not to get money and fame, but to experience becoming, to find out what's inside of you, to make your soul grow. "

—Kurt Vonnegut

So what does any of this have to do with me making art? As I imagined the art sitting unmade in my brand new art studio, with all the supplies I could ever need waiting for me to use them, I realized if I was ever going to make art, I needed to take the same approach I took with writing. I needed to make a commitment, a choice, and I needed to focus on the process, not the final product. If I wanted to be an artist, I needed to do what artists do and show up. To create the same level of accountability and community around my artmaking as I have in the Writing Practice (to compassionately encourage myself to actually make art), I added a weekly artmaking coworking session into my program, the Art Connection

Circle, and then eventually added it to my program for teachers, *Curated Connections*. As the facilitator, I built accountability for the group and myself. As their facilitator, I ensured I was in the space creating with them at least once a week.

After dealing with months of resistance and setting down the baggage that "the art world" laid at my feet, I decided to start an art journal to give myself the freedom to make art without the pressure of "big A" Art. Creating in my art journal, with every art medium I can find within an arm's reach away, has allowed me to find my process, to not to take things so seriously, and to banish any notion of "doing it right" leftover from my college professors grading me according to standards unknown. Just like when I am in the museum and I let works of art bypass my thinking brain and speak directly to the other facets of my being, like my energy, spirit, and emotions, the informality of my art journal allows art to be a practice, an experiment, a place to play, and a place to be with myself.

Cindy Ingram, *Flow*, 2022

I've learned that making art for me is all process. I shut down if I even get a whiff of "what I want this to end up looking like" or "what I want this to be about" energy. My art journal spreads are about starting and letting each step unfold organically. With an open page in my art journal, all I have to do is start making some marks and then follow my intuition each step—looking and letting the composition tell me what to do next. The meaning, if there is one, usually arrives somewhere in the middle or even right at the end, and sometimes the meaning is the joy of creating, and sometimes something deeper appears.

I have been learning to follow and trust my intuition for years, not to stuff down my feelings and my gut reactions, ignoring the red flags and swimming anyway. Working in my art journal, I go through the same feelings. I'll get a little flutter of instinct about an image to collage into the work—sometimes finding it so confusing why I would choose it, but I listen and add it to the collage, finding out later why I chose it as something appears in my life that makes sense. I did say writing makes me feel like a witch. Working in my art journal does too.

My favorite example of this process was this spread:

Cindy Ingram, *Everything You Need*, 2022
Boy image collaged from *Treasure Island* by Robert Louis Stevenson as
illustrated and told in *Classic Adventure Stories*, 1974, Presseburo Junior

I started the spread by choosing colors I wouldn't typically use to see what would happen—green, brown, and yellow—not allowing myself to turn that green to teal, adding in blue to make it feel more like the colors I would choose. As I worked on the background, I started to ponder how the backgrounds often end up being entirely covered by collage and mixed media work. In that meditative process of creating the shapes with watercolor pencil and the patterns using acrylic paint markers, I pondered the importance of the background as a foundation, a place to start, and the information that will guide my intuition to the next steps. As I created this spread, I was intimately meditating on the process of creating my art while in the middle of that process.

Once I finished the background, I was excited to see that the maps my friend had given me for collage purposes were in the same colors I had chosen. I hadn't used them yet because I rarely start with this yellow and green palette. As I cut and glued the map in intuitive shapes, I pondered how my phone's directions are the only rules I follow these days, and even then, I often go off course. After ditching all of the "shoulds" for my business and following my excitement and intuition alone, I've learned that all the information I need is already in me, not in some external expert place. I have all the answers I need in me. I don't need another course, process, or recipe to follow. All I need is me and the process.

I've had the little ship captain image sitting on my desk for several months. He was going to be incorporated into another spread, but he didn't end up making the cut, so he just hung out, waiting to be used. But the yellow hair, brown shirt and wheel, and pop of red perfectly fit my new spread. He even looked lost, like he needed a map. Perfect. Delighted, I found all the yellow and green cars and signs in my collage images book. Once finished, the meaning was clear. All I need to do is follow the guidance inside of me. Use the information I have and listen and trust the small voice inside. And follow the process. The thing I meditated on throughout the whole process of creating this spread ended up being what it was about. It felt like a coincidence, but I know it wasn't. It was the magic of art working with me again. It was chance once again preferring the prepared mind.

✳ ✳ ✳

And I see now that I've been doing this all along. My writing and art-making practices have given me new avenues to be present with myself, to sit with myself as Frida sat with herself in *The Two Fridas*. To be with. Just as I show up to writing practice and my art desk with no expectations but just allowing things to unfold, that's what I have been doing all along. This isn't new, really, just a new manifestation. Art always tells me where to go. Throughout my career, anytime I've gotten stuck—anytime I have felt that I was trying too hard with little results or felt like I was pushing a boulder up a hill, it was because I didn't start with art as my focus. When I open myself to the experience of art, the breadcrumbs appear, and I follow. Art is my divining rod, my pendulum. The art tells me the questions I should ask; the art leads me in ways my head alone cannot.

Change all the times I said art in that last paragraph to "myself," and the meaning stays the same. Art helps me tap into areas of myself inaccessible by other means. I am art, and art is me.

In art

I seek   I find

a clear   a distorted   a magic

window   mirror   microscope   opening

to discover   to understand   to express   to challenge   to accept

how   when   why   that

my mind   my heart   my soul

craves   embodies

wholeness.

Cindy Ingram, *The Protector of Process*, 2023.
Acrylic and paper on canvas

The Protector of Process

Under her fierce watch,
the process unfurls, allows
the truth to appear.

It's funny how process works. Sometimes it appears to be sneaky, but it's not. Once I decided that part three of this book should feature my art, the Art Journal was an obvious choice. But there had to be more, right? And the more clearly would need to be a final chapter featuring an artwork of my own. One piece that would speak for my evolution and credibility as an artist. With this intention, I picked up the art world's baggage I had decided to lay down over the last year (unfortunately and fortunately, the lessons we learn in life, we must learn again and again and again).

If I were to feature my own artwork, I thought it must be a painting, and it must be big. It must be impressive. It must be museum-worthy. It must be as good as the artworks I already feature in this book. And if it is not, I need everyone to know that I know that it isn't as good (it's the Gatorade® spiral all over again). So, I set about painting in the same way I set about my art journal. I stalled. I bought supplies—an easel, more paint, and more canvases. I thought about it and let it sit in my mind for a long time. The pressure of "this will be in the book" weighed heavily on my creativity, keeping me from making my first marks on the canvas. I had an idea of the type of paintings I wanted to make, but I doubted I could actually create paintings that would match these preconceived notions.

Once I finally started painting, I allowed what came through my intuition like I do with my art journal. I followed the nudges and ended up with a completely unexpected result. My first time at my new easel, I painted (randomly and confusingly to me) a white tiger—collaged with book pages like I like to do and painted in colors that my intuition guided me to but that I don't typically use (brown, pink, and off-white). I could tell a whole story about how tigers kept popping up in my life at the time in random contexts, how the colors were inspired by a Scrabble® board and a story that was removed from this book, and how the gold baubles appeared in my mind during a sound bath at my yoga studio. The painting ended up being for me, not a shining accomplishment of my artistic prowess and a way to prove to the world that I am a serious artist. It became a protector for my inner child, who thought having a white tiger for a pet would be pretty badass. It became a lesson in allowing myself to create without pressure. It became a lesson in letting go of the outcome and embracing the process of creating art, not for others but for me.

I then painted a whale and then an atlas moth (which was the feature of the final chapter until the very last minute before handing the book to the designer). Although the transformational metaphor of the moth emerging from the cocoon is one I use throughout the book, my subconscious told me that the Atlas moth wasn't right for that last chapter (and neither was the tiger or the whale). I would see the picture of that moth painting in the final chapter and clench. My mind told me it was not "good enough," but I knew I couldn't do any "better."

There is a reason my first few art journal spreads did not make it into this book. They were rough and experimental. I had never done art journaling before, so I didn't know what I was doing. I didn't start liking what I was making until maybe the eighth page. I enjoyed the process but didn't rush to share the final results. But when it came to this painting, I didn't know what to do. When I don't know what to do—like most of us—I stand still. So I kept the painting in the book, knowing I didn't have time to paint another eight giant canvases to find my groove.

But then, I finally realized the real problem—this painting isn't me. My art felt like it was trying to be something it was not. I felt like I was trying to be something I was not. It wasn't a painting for me. It was a painting for you. It felt like that "smart girl" with all the insecurities about Gatorade® was back, trying to prove to everyone how smart and good she was—begging for their approval. And then, I made the art journal page, inspired by *Girl Before a Mirror*, which ended up as the cover and also in the *Epilogue*, and I loved it. I fucking love that art journal spread so much I can hardly stand it. I wanted to like the art I featured for the last chapter as much as I liked that spread. I wanted it to spark joy and not make me clench. But ultimately, like this entire journey, I wanted it to feel authentic and true because, in the end, that is what this has all been about.

So, I made the collage for the final chapter, which I titled *Emerge*. It's not museum-worthy. No one will buy it or rave over it. It's simple and humble. Crafty even. It's not as grand and impressive as *Night*, *Girl Before a Mirror*, *The Opening*, and *The Anguish of Being*. It's not as clever as *Grow with Progress*, *Jaws*, or *Let Loose the Curious Being*. It's not as emotional or personal as *The Two Fridas*, the two *Self-Portraits*, or *Wrested Heart*. It won't inspire a chapter in someone else's memoir or live on for generations. It is paper, and it will eventually crumble into nothing.

And as I sit here, slowly picking at the glue I can't seem to get off my fingernails, that is enough. I enjoyed making it. I like looking at it. It gave me what art has always given me:

A place to feel at home.

A place to feel present.

A place where I feel like me.

A place to feel whole.

A place to be whole.

My art is enough, because I am enough.

Cindy Ingram, *Emerge*, 2023. Mixed media on paper

Emerge

Possibility
exists in the connection
between art and self

I've compared art with magic many times throughout this book. And to me, it always has had that magical quality, but I would have never called the work that I do magic. Magic is one of those things in the "not safe" category to consider as a smart person. Still, as I come to a place where I put that *wrested heart* back into my chest, where I become unapologetic about who I am and who I want to be, where I start listening to my own intuition, where I feel my feelings instead of stuff them down, things have started to happen that just feel magical. Not Harry Potter wand magic, but the magic of synchronicity, the magic of intuition, of things falling into place and happening in ways I can't explain. Once the noise of shame and self-doubt quieted, I can finally hear that soft voice inside, and I now trust the wisdom of that voice—my intuition.

Listening to your intuition may sound easy, but it took sixteen chapters and forty-two years of growth to learn how to truly listen to my own (and I am still learning). Sometimes your intuition tells you things you do not want to hear. It tells you something you have been avoiding for a reason. It shakes you up, and if you actually listen, you get the call to completely shake up the business you have been growing for the last decade, digital brick by digital brick. Or to potentially blow up your marriage. Or to upset your mom. It's easier sometimes to just not pay attention and just keep swimming, so you don't have to face the feelings that come up when you do listen. But eventually, the pain of ignoring that voice becomes worse than the pain listening would cause, and that's when it is time to take action.

✳ ✳ ✳

Throughout this book, I've pondered on the journey a moth takes from caterpillar to cocoon to moth. When does it know to go through each stage? I'm completely aware of and self-conscious about how cliche it is to talk about transformation with this metaphor, but I think it is a cliche for a reason; it is an apt metaphor. But I also think it has its faults and some unrealistic expectations built in. Just as I expressed with the linear path of the stairs in *Grow With Progress*, this metaphor implies that there is only one final destination, when we all know that we are in an ever constant state of evolving, changing, transformation, and becoming. For this chapter, I vulnerably use my own artwork as the anchor. In this mixed media collage, there is a cocoon hanging from a branch collaged with text from some of my favorite books. Along with collaged butterflies and moths, the artwork includes the haiku from the beginning of the *Caterpillars, Butterflies, and Flowers* chapter.

✳ ✳ ✳

Running a business is a rollercoaster, and the biggest ride of my business life began in March 2020. The beginning of the pandemic was a turning point in a lot of people's lives, but for me, instead of slowing or shutting down, I sprung into action. As students and teachers made the dramatic and sudden switch to online learning, my business Art Class Curator was primed with the solution to the problem because it is dedicated to teaching with works of art rather than art supplies. We offered an online conference for art teachers and a distance learning curriculum within weeks of the pandemic's beginning. In the new school year, we offered a Hybrid Learning art curriculum to support teachers who had to weave in and out of teaching online for the 2021-22 school year. It was the exact right product for the exact right time.

The following year, big things happened for the business as we served teachers in their time of need. New opportunities were offered, and my company grew by leaps and bounds. It was an exciting time. After years of running a business, it was so satisfying to see my work in the world flow so beautifully and impact teachers and students worldwide. People were not only paying us but also thanking us as they handed over the money. I was so energized by the influx of excitement in my business that all the red flags and burnout I had been experiencing with "Bruce" (*dun-nuh... dun-nuh...*) were forgotten for a while.

The growth of Art Class Curator during that first year of the pandemic was life-changing. I saw all of my dreams come true right before my eyes. Everything I was striving for was coming to fruition—personally and professionally. In 2020, the yearly income from the business tripled. Personally, I eliminated my credit card debt, I traded in my rickety, doors-sticking, shit-gray minivan for a nicer car, and we finally got out of the rental market and bought a house that ticked off most of our wants (I finally had my own office!). We finally got out ahead of our finances for the first time. On the business side, I had been working on "scaling" my business for years, trying to grow—getting more students from across the world to connect with artworks and more teachers to see the power of this work. One goal was to get more districts to pay for our program rather than individual teachers because teachers shouldn't have to pay for curriculum, and the pandemic brought infusions of government funds into school districts to do just that. District sales increased by at least 500 percent and felt natural and easy.

Art Class Curator was growing and growing fast. At the time, I may have likened myself to the majestic moth (the largest known moth is the Atlas moth which has a wingspan of nearly ten inches!), experiencing exciting success after years and years of work, but looking back, I now know that I was the caterpillar. The caterpillar that eventually becomes the Atlas moth has to eat enough sustenance to survive not only its current life as a caterpillar and for its time in the cocoon but also has to eat enough to sustain its short life as a full-grown moth. I was eating up all the opportunities, saying yes to everything, and growing as big and fast as I could in all the excitement.

The growth also got Art Class Curator onto some radars, and we were approached to write a curriculum for an art supply company. They made life-changing promises of sales, and we were all in. We threw ourselves into creating this curriculum, knowing that this was the thing that would send Art Class Curator into the stratosphere. This would make us that big company attractive to districts and reach the most teachers and students. I made two of my part-time positions full-time and hired a slew of teacher contractors, and we got to work creating this curriculum that would earn us that seven-figure income that I had always had my eye on as an ambitious entrepreneur. I knew this was it. This is what I had been working towards for years, finally breaking through to the massive success that I always thought was possible.

By Spring 2021 however, everyone, especially teachers, was exhausted from dealing with the pandemic for months longer than they ever thought it would go, with no end in sight. That school year, art teachers were being forced to go through extraordinary measures just to do their jobs—some were teaching outside only, some were still at home, many were forced to go onto "art on a cart," and many art classes were just canceled. Some art teachers became grade-level teachers so schools could reduce class sizes. When we launched our brand new curriculum in January of 2021 after having been promised a million in sales by the partner company, the curriculum fell into the ears of teachers who were burnt out, exhausted, and in survival mode.

And I was there too. After months of eating up all the new opportunities, my caterpillar body had grown too big and became too hard to manage. Truth be told, it was not fun writing that curriculum. Because of those income projections and the amazing opportunity presented to us to reach more students and teachers, I pushed past how challenging, stressful, and expensive that curriculum was to create, believing it would be worth it in the end. I ignored the uneasiness and anxiety that had settled in my body. The moment that stands out most in my head is me sitting on the couch editing lesson plans while crying because going into my office caused too much anxiety. Something felt wrong, but I was pushing through anyway.

I wasn't listening to that wise voice inside.

This curriculum would be the ticket to getting my business to a place where I could work on projects I wanted to work on and outsource the parts of my work that I was ready to let go of. Even before Covid, I was starting to feel disconnected. I remember sitting in a circle of other women entrepreneurs at a retreat a month before Covid, saying, "I'm not having fun in my business anymore. I miss the fun and energy it once had." The bigger my business grew, the more the work became less about my passion and more about growing. The business became about standardization and branding and systems and team and communication. It became about forty-five-minute phone calls with district admins and going to the notary to fill out a form. It became about scaling and growth. And as it grew, the more and more I started to get those nudges again that maybe this wasn't what I wanted (*dun-nuh... dun-nuh...*). I had business coaches helping me with strategies to sell to school districts that would send me into panic attacks because it was further and further from the work that truly lit me up.

❋ ❋ ❋

The caterpillar runs on instinct and eats non-stop; nearly every second of its life is spent eating. It knows, somehow, that it's preparing for something else. I imagine as it grows bigger and bigger and eats more and more, its body sends nudges when it is nearing time to stop, but it keeps pushing until it is forced to stop. It keeps pushing until it can't continue as a caterpillar any longer. As I strayed further from my creativity, the nudges became more than nudges. They became big glaring messages saying, "It is time to stop NOW!"

Though it made some sales, that big curriculum project was mostly a failure. It didn't make the money we had counted on, and the financial risk I took to make it happen did not pay out in the end. I had to lay off or cut the hours of my beloved staff and cut expenses way down. Having to lay off two team members felt like a free fall. All along, I was banking on the curriculum working out so that I could hire more team members to manage the parts of the business that were stressing me out, but really I was trying to hide from what I knew deep down about the type of work I wanted to do. The big lesson in the whole situation was that I needed to pay more attention to those intuitive nudges of anxiety, the resistance I felt about certain tasks, and the stress I felt with too many voices vying for my attention.

For a person whose whole existence is centered around accomplishment and success—being no less than the best—this was a hard fall. I felt immense shame and guilt toward my team and those I had to let go, toward the art supply company who let me down and who I let down, and toward my family. My mental health was in a desperate state—depressed and anxious. I couldn't work or do a lot of anything. If I saw an art teacher post on Facebook, I'd have to scroll fast to get it off my screen because it caused so much anxiety. I completely stopped.

> " The credit belongs to the man who is actually in
> the arena, whose face is marred by dust and
> sweat and blood; who strives valiantly; who errs,
> who comes short again and again, because
> there is no effort without error and shortcoming;
> but who does actually strive to do the deeds;
> who knows great enthusiasms, the great devotions; who
> spends himself in a worthy cause;
> who at the best knows in the end the triumph
> of high achievement, and who at the worst,
> if he fails, at least fails while daring greatly. "
> — Theodore Roosevelt

I was battered and broken on the arena floor, confused by the contradictions of pride from my great successes and the shame from the failed aftermath. I had fallen and didn't know how to get back up again. Or maybe I knew how to get back up, but I didn't want to admit that getting up meant changing everything. Deep in burnout, there was no way I could plow through the resistance I was feeling anymore. It was time for me, overstuffed and overworked, to enter my cocoon.

I completely stopped working and focused on how to heal. I surrounded myself with support as I figured it out. I leaned into my family, coaches, and friends. At home, I spent a lot of time on the couch in my own cocoon of pillows and blankets. I embraced the space I needed in that cocoon I made on the couch, but what really needed attention was this underlying feeling that something wasn't right. There was a missing piece, something I knew in my heart and body that my mind hadn't fully understood. There was a yearning for something deeper in my business—more intimate connections, more work with teachers as individuals, not just as educators. More engaging people with art, rather than about art or how to teach art. There was a message in all of this. I needed to discover something bigger and greater, and there was no way to rush that process. Time and space were what I needed.

When the moth is in the cocoon, disassembling itself to become something new, does it know what it is becoming?

❋ ❋ ❋

My philosophy on art has morphed over the years of running this business. With every art interaction, every minute spent in front of art, it's become clearer to me—easier to understand and share with others, like lights being turned on in a dark room. It started as a child, this thing I loved, but I didn't know why. Crying at the art of Disney® movies and being knocked over by art at my first museum. I knew I loved art, so I chased it. I chased the feeling it gave me and wanted others to feel that too. So I studied it. I learned how to teach it in ways that I wasn't taught. I taught art. I helped teachers teach it. I relished the teachers' stories of the engaged classrooms and powerful lessons, but I felt disconnected from their experience the further I got from the classroom. I wanted to be a part of the intimate art conversations. I wanted to be in the room where it happened. The bigger my company grew, the less work with the actual art I got to do. Writing lessons about art for others to teach no longer gave me the thrill it once did.

As my goals started to be reached—more district clients, a bigger team—it was hard to realize that this place I had hustled and strived for wasn't what I wanted. Like you've spent your life dreaming of living on the beach, and once you finally get your beach house, you realize you can't stand the sand everywhere, the humidity is miserable, and you have hurricanes to deal with. I had spent the last seven years building a business I was no longer in love with, but I had been stuffing down that inkling for years.

But underneath all that, I knew something deeper was waiting to be discovered. I spent a year visiting art museums, reading, and receiving coaching and healing sessions. I started making art again. I started writing a book about art education, thinking it would reconnect me with my mission at Art Class Curator. This book started as a book with footnotes and research about why and how to teach with works of art. I learned that I had just as much resistance to writing about art education as I did about the rest of my work in art education. Trying to convince people about this magical connection to art—this feeling I get with art that overwhelms me and takes me over. This feeling that connects me to my humanity, my spirit, and myself. It's bigger than "appreciating" or "critiquing" art. It's bigger than learning about art. It's bigger than developing students' critical thinking skills and social and emotional learning. It's so much more.

How do I stop *telling* people about its power, and how do I actually *show* them?

I understood the feeling art gave me, but I still couldn't name it.

How do you teach something you can't name?

If my unnamable feeling in front of a work of art is what I am meant to share with the world, and I believe it is my true purpose and magic, how would I even do that?

How do you show someone the inside of your heart?

How do you show them what can happen in front of a work of art? Is it even possible?

And then...something clicked. Art has not been my only lifelong obsession. Behind the scenes, I have been working on myself. I'm always reading a self-help book. I delight in psychology and ideas. I love studying why people do what they do and how to be whole and healed. My sister, who follows me on Goodreads and doesn't read every self-help book she can find, jokes to me, "Are you perfect yet?" But really, it's not about becoming perfect.

It's about feeling good.

It's about quieting the inner critic, silencing the mean voice telling me I'm not good enough.

It's about healing the trauma of my past.

It's about understanding and accepting my neuroses and sensitivities.

It's about learning to trust, like, and love myself.

It's about making me a better communicator—a better friend, sister, daughter, mother, and wife.

It's about slowly releasing the inner burdens and anxieties one by one that keep me from being the best and most content version of myself.

It's about taking care of myself at the highest level possible.

It's about being whole.

Perfect is impossible because perfect is not a thing. It doesn't exist. But what does exist is the ability to feel better about who I am today than I felt yesterday. It's possible to love myself more today than I did yesterday. It's possible to take a stand for breaking the cycle of the patriarchy, questioning assumptions, stories, societal norms, and expectations. It's possible to find my place amidst the world's expectations of me. Because every book I read, every artwork I experience, every conversation I have, and every artwork I make or word I write makes me a more whole-hearted, peaceful, and fully alive version of myself.

So what clicked? I realized what looking at art was for me.

Art is my meditation

> my challenger
> my refuge
> my sacred journey
> my spiritual practice
> my meditation cushion
> my temple
> my altar
> my pew

Art is one of my tools for self-development, just as much as all those books I've read. I have said over the years that I don't look at art to learn about the art. I look at art to learn about myself. I look at art to learn about the world and my place in it. I look at art to fully understand and embody who I am, who I want to be, and how I want to be.

✳ ✳ ✳

As inspired as I was by these new thoughts of where my work could take me, I was still in the goo of my cocoon, in the bug soup as my coach and friend Allison Crow calls it. As I started to reassemble myself into a whole form after being sidelined by layered feelings of guit, shame, and grief, I began to play with this idea that art connection is my magic. I started to dream of what was possible if I fully leaned into my deep emotional connection to art and let everything else go. In the cocoon, my caterpillar now knows it can't return to the form it once was. It was time to make wings.

I still can't name the unnameable, but I realized I can combine my love of art with my love of self-development to create an experience for people like nothing they have ever encountered. I know from first-hand experience the magic that happens when you put people in front of a work of art. Art provides a safety net that releases people from the burden of vulnerability. It anchors the choppy seas of difficult emotions and hard topics.

So, with this realization, I started the hesitant and risky journey of changing course. Art Class Curator still works with teachers and offers the same programs, but I have shifted my priority to something even deeper. I scrapped the serious, studious art education book I had started writing, let go of the research assistant I hired to do the parts of the book that I was resisting, and started the one you are reading now. I started making art. I also created the first *Art Connection Circle* to experiment with the idea that you could use art as a tool for self-development.

The *Art Connection Circle* is an intimate group program allowing us to experience art as I have modeled in this book. We interpret and discuss the artwork and, at the same time, find ourselves in it. We learn about who we are and do it in a safe and supportive environment of others doing the same deep work. We allow the art to hold our vulnerability and deepen our understanding of ourselves. In the first run of this program, seven beautiful humans took a chance on this unnameable, indescribable experience because they had faith in my work. What transpired was truly magical. It was the most connected, fulfilling experience of my life, and I wish there were adequate words to describe the energy and love in that Zoom room.

❋ ❋ ❋

As I looked back at my life in the moments after the first Circle wrapped up—warm in the glow of love and connection, I saw every thread leading to that very moment. Every decision, every win, every mistake, every risk, every tear, every disappointment. This is what it was all for.

I am art and art is me.

This is me   emerging from the cocoon—colorful and bold, ready to test my wings.

This is me   discovering my magic.

This is me   crying in the movie theater during *Circle of Life* in 8th grade, feeling the call to something deeper.

This is me   witnessing both my pain and passion in *Girl Before a Mirror* as an insecure, anxious twenty-three-year-old.

This is me   repressing my unsafe feelings—feeling them burn through my heart, skin, and clothes like the first of *The Two Fridas*.

This is me   sitting vulnerably next to my mother as in Joffe's *Self-Portrait*—experiencing the contradictions of the power of my body as a mother alongside society's constraining expectations of it.

This is me   feeling the over-stimulation of Bacon's *Self-Portrait* one day and the peace and wonder of *Night* the next.

This is me   learning to feel those feelings, to release the tension in my body and let them flow like in *The Opening*.

This is me   knowing these feelings mean I'm alive—a human experiencing both the ecstasy and the *Anguish of Being*.

This is me   dropping a message on a ribbon into the *River of Time* to my long-deceased father, releasing his hold on my heart.

This is me   staring into the painted eyes at the Leopold Museum in Vienna feeling connected to my humanness in a way that I could never possibly explain.

This is me   working tirelessly towards my mission of healing myself and tirelessly toward my mission of bringing art into people's hearts.

This is me   making art and writing poems again—rediscovering parts of myself long buried.

This is me   cradling my *Wrested Heart* and gently pulling it back into my body where it belongs.

This is me   whole and unbroken.

This is me   as art.

Art has always been pulling me towards something, guiding me somewhere unknown, and I have been following the breadcrumbs my whole life. Art has led me to heal myself and now to help heal others. And all I have to do now is listen.

As I tunnel through my memory to
each art museum and artwork I have witnessed
in my life, artworks in the thousands by this point,
more than I can possibly remember,
I see me as I shift and grow,
different versions of myself suspended in time.
Fully present and open
in ways I never could name.
Fully accepting myself more than
I ever could in the real world.
It is a relief to show up
as I am
to the art—whole and unbroken—and for that to be
enough.
In front of art,
I feel my presence. My mindfulness. My meditation. My moments
of awe, of delight, of introspection, of curiosity, of love.
Of stillness.
When I am with art
I want
        nothing more,
I need
        nothing more.
I am who I need to be
to experience the art
today.
The art and I
will never meet again in this same way,
because although the art remains still,
I am new.

Ingram, C. (2023). *Girl Out of the Mirror* [mixed media on paper].

Epilogue:
Return to Wholeness

Mirror for a girl,
Art is about being whole.
A return to me.

The poetry isn't lost on me that over the last year, I have created two books simultaneously: the book you are reading and my art journal. Both books are finishing at about the same time. Both books have profoundly changed me. Both have opened up new possibilities for my future. Both have challenged, consoled, and lifted me up in ways I could not have imagined.

I wrote poems and let you read them. I made art and let you see it.

Both the processes of writing and making art over the last year have changed my identity. I was an educator passionate about art, a business owner who is passionate about art and who also writes some, and now I am Writer, and I am Artist. That shift in identity has changed everything, and as I close both books for the last time, I don't see it as an ending but a beginning. It is an opening. I am ready to see where my intuition guides me next and where art leads me.

What is possible with full self-trust?

What is possible when I accept and love myself as I am?

What is possible with wholeness?

> 66 Trusting yourself means living out
> what you already know to be true. 99
> — Cheryl Strayed in *Tiny Beautiful Things*

❋ ❋ ❋

Creating this artwork, inspired by Picasso's *Girl Before a Mirror*, I allow that girl on the inside to expand into the space—out of the mirror and into herself. I now see my depth in those beautiful jewel tones instead of the shame and mystery I once saw there. The addition of the patterns cut from water and space show my connection to the expansiveness of life, and the thick orange tear, which once represented my deep sadness, glitters with gold to show the importance of my feelings. I have learned through this process that feelings are meant to be felt—it means I am a human and an artist. I am happier than I have ever been, not in spite of my feelings but because of them. Those intense feelings allow me to respond to art with my whole body; they are my fire and fuel. They make me who and how I am, and I finally know who that is.

When I look in the mirror now, I am not broken into pieces like Picasso's girl. I am made of many parts; yes, these are pieces of me. But I am not broken, and I never was. Wholeness, I have discovered, is not an arrival to a place of being fixed or of having it all put together and perfect, but a process of accepting and loving who you are now, learning and re-learning over and over again. I am a kaleidoscope of feelings, energies, wild edges, talents, sensitivities, frustrations, vulnerabilities, personality, and contradictions. Through my explorations of art and self, I have come to love and accept the girl in the mirror. She is so much more than I once thought she had to be.

Art has helped me come home to myself. I know in the future that I will go through bug soup again, and again, and again. I will struggle. I will fail. I will nestle back into the cocoon. I will feel all the feelings. And I will also fly myself home because home is me. Art is me.

Cento Poem: Art Is About Being Whole

A cento poem is a work of poetry that is composed of various lines taken from different poems. The word "cento" is derived from a Latin word meaning "patchwork garment"—and a cento poem is just that— patchwork poetry (also known as a 'collage poem'). At the end of my writing sessions, I've often said "this is like a puzzle," but now I see that the writing of this book resembles the collages I do in art journals more than a puzzle. I've brought this book out into the world by taking into account both the little details and the big picture at the same time—looking for the threads that tie my story together while keeping each chapter distinct. Just like I look for the right paper, line, color, or media to add to the overall picture, writing this book included collaging together art, metaphor, and narrative to accurately describe feelings and transformations that can't easily be explained with words. This cento poem below, inspired by the ending poem in Maggie Smith's incredible *You Could Make this Place Beautiful*, is a beautiful collage of this book, showing my path to wholeness through art.

Art is About Being Whole

I am wrong. I am broken into pieces like Picasso's girl,
shame as the mortar
between not acceptable and not enough,
trying to hide the mess within.
I can break the cycle and start a new story:
what if I could feel light, happy, and free?
I could feel the change stirring—solid in my body—
I needed love and connection to heal my deep wounds of disconnection.

How does [one] take the first step into a new life?
Growth is an up-and-down roller coaster.
It's an M.C. Escher trippy illustration or the stairs changing at Hogwarts.

After living in chaotic internal anguish for so long, I fought hard
for this ordinary, stable life.
Having the perfect job, the perfect location, the perfect belongings,
the perfect friends, the perfect weight—
all of it would equal the perfect me.

Living that full vital life of my dreams,
there was an undercurrent of anxiety simmering
underneath my policy of "just keep swimming."
I was avoiding thinking and feeling,
aware of the red flags and the ominous music playing
beneath the surface,
not ready to listen.

[And yet] the answers could no longer be found outside of me;
I had to go beneath the surface.
I had to open myself up,
allow the swirl to clean out the last remnant of old shame.
[I] surrendered to [my] awe, letting it contort
[my] body into an uncomfortable position to get a better look
at [my] curiosity.
In one moment, I was past, present, and future.
It was a place of peace, compassion, and understanding.
That's what art does.
It allows [me] to expand
and recognize myself
in a place that may have seemed
forbidden, irresponsible, or unattainable.
It doesn't make me feel small; it makes me feel like a miracle.
When I emotionally react to a work of art, I am connected
with something bigger than myself.
For a moment, I am connected
to that artist, another person from another time and another place.
I feel I am not alone in the world;
I understand my place.
I am valuable and unbroken.

Cutting through all the noise,
I can hear myself now.
I am the art, and the art is me.

Continue Connecting With Art

Free Downloads – Art Connection and Book Club Guide

Thank you so much for reading this book. If this work resonates with you and you want to keep exploring your connection to art, I invite you to download the art connection guide to accompany the artworks in this book at artandself.com/book. The guide will lead you through your own discovery and connection to the works. Also available at that same link is a book club guide with a twist—use this book with your book club, and instead of a traditional discussion of the book, I will show you how to weave art discussions into your gathering.

How to Connect with Cindy

Email Me
cindy@artandself.com

Connect with Me on Social Media
https://linktr.ee/artandself

Listen to the Art and Self Podcast
https://artandself.com/podcast

Join an Art Connection Circle
https://artandself.com/circle

Are you an art teacher?

Join *Curated Connections* for art connection curriculum and training.
https://artclasscurator.com/join

References

Billboard Hot 100: Week of September 24, 1988. (1988, September 24). Billboard. https://www.billboard.com/charts/hot100/1988-09-24/

Brown, B. (2013, January 15). *Shame vs. guilt.* Brene Brown. https://brenebrown.com/articles/2013/01/15/shame-v-guilt/

Campbell, J. & Moyers, B. (1991). *The power of myth.* Bantam Doubleday Dell Publishing Group.

Cary Grant quotes, witticisms, one liners and knock-out dialogue. (2022, November 4). PBS. https://www.pbs.org/wnet/americanmasters/cary-grant-quotable-cary/618/

Chernick, K. (2020, January 3). Think you know Frida Kahlo? Think again. Here are the Mexican painter's most under-the-radar artworks—Ranked. *Artnet.* https://news.artnet.com/art-world/frida-kahlo-portraits-ranked-1736778

Cochrane, T. (1991). Life is a highway [Song]. On *Mad mad world.* EMI Music Canada.

Cummins, J. (2020). *American Dirt.* Flatiron Books.

Edwards, E. (2022). *Natalie Wadlington: Places that grow* [Exhibition]. Dallas Contemporary, Dallas, TX, United States.

Egan, J. (2022). *The Candy House.* Scribner.

Foa'i, Mancina, M. & Miranda, L. (2016). I am Moana (Song of the ancestors) [Recorded by A. Cravalho R. House]. On *Moana: Original motion picture soundtrack.* Walt Disney.

Gottlieb, L. (2019). *Maybe you should talk to someone: A therapist, her therapist, and our lives revealed.* Harper.

Heckerling, A. (Director). (1995). *Clueless* [Film]. Paramount Pictures.

Heroic Century: The Museum of Modern Art masterpieces, 200 paintings and sculptures [Exhibition]. (2003-2004). The Museum of Fine Arts Houston, Houston, TX, United States.

It is not the critic who counts. (2011, January 18). Theodore Roosevelt Conservation Partnership. https://www.trcp.org/2011/01/18/it-is-not-the-critic-who-counts

John, E. & Rice, T. (1994). Circle of life [Recorded by C. Twillie and Lebo M]. On *The lion king original motion picture soundtrack.* Walt Disney.

Karnes, A. (2021). *Women painting women* [Exhibition]. The Modern Art Museum of Fort Worth, Fort Worth, TX, United States.

King, L. (2020). *Writers & lovers.* Blackstone Publishing.

Kingsolver, B. (2022). *Demon copperhead.* Harper.

Klune, T. J. (2020). *House in the cerulean sea.* Tor.

Koenig, J. (2012, July 22). *Sonder.* The Dictionary of Obscure Sorrows. https://www.dictionaryofobscuresorrows.com/post/23536922667/sonder

Lamott, A. (1995). *Bird by bird: Some instructions on writing and life.* Knopf Doubleday Publishing Group.

Louis Pasteur quotes. (n.d.). Goodreads. https://www.goodreads.com/authorquotes/692216.Louis_Pasteur

Martin, M. (2021, October 22). *A river of time: Pamela Nelson creates art with ribbons of grief.* Dallas Doing Good. https://dallasdoinggood.com/a-river-of-time-pamela-nelson-creates-art-with-ribbons-of-grief

McLaren, K. (2010). *The language of emotions: What your feelings are trying to tell you.* Sounds True.

Napolitano, A. (2020). *Dear Edward.* The Dial Press.

Oliver, M. (2019). *Devotions: The selected poems of Mary Oliver.* Penguin Press.

Pablo Picasso quotes. (n.d.). BrainyQuote.com. https://www.brainyquote.com/quotes/pablo_picasso_104106

Powers, R. (2021). *Bewilderment.* W. W. Norton & Company.

Ramaci, T., Bellini, D., Presti, G., & Santisi, G. (2019). Psychological flexibility and mindfulness as predictors of individual outcomes in hospital health workers. *Frontiers in psychology, 10,* 1302. https://doi.org/10.3389/fpsyg.2019.01302

Rumi quotes. (n.d.). Goodreads. https://goodreads.com/author/quotes/875661.Rumi

Safran Foer, J. (2006). *Extremely Loud and Incredibly Close.* Mariner Books.

Santon, A. & Unkrich, L. (Directors). (2002). *Finding Nemo* [Film]. Pixar Animation Studios; Walt Disney Pictures.

Searing, L. (2018, January 1). *The big number: 45 million Americans go on a diet each year.* The Washington Post. https://www.washingtonpost.com/national/health-science/the-big-number-45-million-americans-go-on-a-diet-each-year/2017/12/29/04089aec-ebdd-11e7-b698-91d4e35920a3_story.html

Smith, M. (2023). *You Could Make This Place Beautiful.* Atria/One Signal Publishers.

Speilberg, S. (Director). (1975). *Jaws* [Film]. Zanuck Brown Productions; Universal Pictures.

Strayed, S. (2022). *Tiny beautiful things (10th anniversary edition): Advice from dear sugar.* Knopf Doubleday Publishing Group.

Usher, S. (2021, November 5). *Make your soul grow: Kurt Vonnegut, 84, writes to some students.* Letters of Note. https://news.lettersofnote.com/p/make-your-soul-grow

Van der Kolk, B. A. (2015). *The body keeps the score: brain, mind, and body in the healing of trauma.* New York, New York, Penguin Books.

Van Pelt, S. (2022). *Remarkably bright creatures.* Ecco.

West, L. (2016). *Shrill: Notes from a loud woman.* Hachette Books.

What to know about an adrenaline rush. (2021, April 27). WebMD. https://www.webmd.com/a-to-z-guides/what-to-know-adrenaline-rush

Wilkerson, C. (2022). *Black cake.* Ballantine Books.

Williams, J. (1975). Main title (Theme from "Jaws") [Song]. On Jaws (Music from the original motion picture soundtrack). Geffen Records.

Wipplinger, H. P. (2019-2023). Vienna 1990 [Exhibtion]. Leopold Museum, Vienna, Austria.

Zevin, G. (2022). *Tomorrow, and tomorrow, and tomorrow.* Knopf.

Art Featured in
Art Is About Being Whole

The details and images of art journal collages and mixed media used throughout the book as design elements were created by Cindy Ingram from *Art Journal, Volumes 1–3* and are not specifically cited below.

In order of appearance:

Swoon. (2011). *Thalassa* [block print on paper with hand painted colors in acrylic gouache, mounted to wooden panels]. Buffalo AKG Art Museum, Buffalo, NY, United States. https://buffaloakg.org/artworks/202013-thalassa

Picasso, P. (1932, March 14). *Girl before a mirror* [oil on canvas]. The Museum of Modern Art, New York, NY, United States. https://www.moma.org/collection/works/78311

Kahlo, F. (1939). *The two Fridas (Las dos Fridas)* [oil on canvas]. Museo Nacional de Arte Moderno, Mexico City, Mexico. https://mam.inba.gob.mx/

Monet, C. (1900). *Water lily pond* [oil on canvas]. The Art Institute of Chicago, Chicago, IL, United States. https://www.artic.edu/artworks/87088/water-lily-pond

Joffe, C. (2020). *Self-portrait naked with my mother II* [oil on board]. Victoria Miro. https://online.victoria-miro.com/chantaljoffe-london2021/

Bacon, F. (1956). *Self-portrait* [oil on canvas]. The Modern Art Museum of Fort Worth, Fort Worth, TX, United States. https://collection.themodern.org/objects/201/selfportrait

de Saint Phalle, N. (1999). *The three graces* [fiberglass and mosaic]. National Museum of Women in the Arts, Washington, DC, United States.

Merian, M.S. (1705). *Caterpillars, butterflies and flower* [hand-colored etching and engraving]. Minneapolis Institute of Art, Minneapolis, MN, United States. https://collections.artsmia.org/art/7368/caterpillars-maria-sibylla-merian

Johansson, E. (2021). *Grow with progress* [photograph]. Erik Johansson. https://www.erikjo.com/work/grow-with-progress

Kastel, R. (1975). *Jaws* [unknown media]. Roger Kastel. http://www.rogerkastel.com/

Colquhoun, I. (1942). *Dance of the nine opals* [oil on canvas]. Tate, London, United Kingdom. https://www.bridgemanimages.com/en/colquhoun/the-dance-of-the-nine-opals-1942-oil-on-canvas/oil-on-canvas/asset/390511

Lipschutz, P. (1999). *Wrested heart* [oil on canvas]. Private collection.

Chapin, A. (2020-2021). *The opening* [oil on canvas]. Aleah Chapin. http://www.aleahchapin.com/202021/the-opening

Wadlington, N. (2022). *Night* [oil on canvas]. Natalie Wadlington. https://www.nataliewadlington.com/

Raya, M. (2000). *The anguish of being and the nothingness of the universe* [acrylic on canvas]. Museum of Fine Arts Houston, Houston, TX, United States. https://emuseum.mfah.org/objects/76946/the-anguish-of-being-and-the-nothingness-of-the-universe

Nelson, P. (2021). *River of time* [woven ribbons]. Pamela Nelson. https://pamelahnelson.com/. Photograph by C. Ingram.

Hrdlicka, A. (1964). *Portrait Oskar Kokoschka II (detail)* [bronze]. Leopold Museum, Vienna, Austria. Photograph by C. Ingram.

Schiele, E. (1912). *Mother and child (detail)* [oil on wood]. Leopold Museum, Vienna, Austria.

Kalvach, R. (1907-08). *Holy family (detail)* [oil and tempera on wood]. Leopold Museum, Vienna, Austria.

Kokoschka, O. (1910). *Poster 'The Storm' (detail)* [color lithograph on paper, facsimile]. Leopold Museum, Vienna, Austria.

Schönberg, A. (1910). *Gaze (Karl Kraus) (detail)* [oil on cardboard]. Leopold Museum, Vienna, Austria.

Romako, A. (1885). *Portrait of Isabella Reisser (detail)* [oil on canvas]. Leopold Museum, Vienna, Austria.

Schiele, E. (1912). *Mourning woman (detail)* [oil on wood]. Leopold Museum, Vienna, Austria.

Schiele, E. (1912). *Self-portrait with raised bare shoulder (detail)* [oil on wood]. Leopold Museum, Vienna, Austria.

Klimt, G. (1883). *Head study of a girl from Haná (detail)* [oil on wood]. Leopold Museum, Vienna, Austria.

Kokoschka, O. (1909). *Pietà. Poster for his play 'Murderer, Hope of Women' at the Internationale Kunstschau, Vienna (detail)* [color lithograph on paper]. Leopold Museum, Vienna, Austria.

Birkle, A. (1923). *Man with fur cap (My brother the animal) (detail)* [oil on canvas]. Leopold Museum, Vienna, Austria.

Schönberg, A. (c. 1910). *Emil Hertzka (detail)* [oil on cardboard]. Leopold Museum, Vienna, Austria.

Schiele, E. (1910). *Portrait of Poldi Lodzinsky (detail)* [oil on canvas]. Leopold Museum, Vienna, Austria.

Schönberg, A. (c. 1910). *Christ (detail)* [oil on cardboard]. Leopold Museum, Vienna, Austria.

Schönberg, A. (1910). *Mathilde Schönberg (detail)* [oil on canvas]. Leopold Museum, Vienna, Austria.

Schiele, E. (1918). *Lovers (unfinished) (detail)* [oil on canvas]. Leopold Museum, Vienna, Austria.

von Lenbach, F. (c. 1870). *Franziska von Wertheimstein (detail)* [oil on wood]. Leopold Museum, Vienna, Austria.

Kalvach, R. (1907-08). *Holy family (detail)* [oil and tempera on wood]. Leopold Museum, Vienna, Austria.

Kokoschka, O. (1922). *Self-portrait at the easel (detail)* [oil on canvas]. Leopold Museum, Vienna, Austria.

Schiele, E. (1915). *Mother with Two Children II (detail)* [oil on canvas]. Leopold Museum, Vienna, Austria.

Kurzweil, M. (1907). *Female Nude with Mask Before the Mirror (detail)* [oil on canvas]. Leopold Museum, Vienna, Austria.

Schiele, E. (1915). *Transfiguration (The blind II) (detail)* [oil, opaque color on canvas]. Leopold Museum, Vienna, Austria.

Klimt, G. (1915). *Death and life (detail)* [oil on canvas]. Leopold Museum, Vienna, Austria.

Klimt, G. (c. 1896). *The blind man (detail)* [oil on canvas]. Leopold Museum, Vienna, Austria.

Schiele, E. (1910). *Seated nude (Self-portrait) (detail)* [oil, opaque color on canvas]. Leopold Museum, Vienna, Austria.

Schönberg, A. (1910). *Gustav Mahler (detail)* [oil on cardboard]. Leopold Museum, Vienna, Austria.

Schönberg, A. (1910). *Alexander Zemlinksy (detail)* [oil on board]. Leopold Museum, Vienna, Austria.

Klimt, G. (1907-08). *Lady with hat on a red background (detail)* [oil on canvas]. Leopold Museum, Vienna, Austria.

Shaden, B. (2015). *Let loose the curious being* [photograph]. Brooke Shaden. https://brookeshaden.com/gallery/?page=2&title=let_loose_the_curious_being

Sikander, S. (2009). *Mary Magdalene* [ink and gouache on prepared paper]. Metropolitan Opera. https://www.metopera.org/visit/exhibitions/past-exhibitions/something-about-mary/

Ingram, C. (2022). *Whale* [mixed media on paper].

Ingram, C. (2023). *Strange and Sweet World* [mixed media on paper].

Ingram, C. (2023). *I am Moana* [mixed media on paper].

Ingram, C. (2023). *Magic Woman* [mixed media on paper].

Ingram, C. (2022). *Goldilocks* [mixed media on paper].

Ingram, C. (2022). *Flow* [mixed media on paper].

Ingram, C. (2022). *Everything You Need* [mixed media on paper].

Ingram, C. (2023). *Protector of Process* [acrylic and paper on canvas].

Ingram, C. (2023). *Emerge* [mixed media on paper].

Ingram, C. (2023). *Girl Out of the Mirror* [mixed media on paper].

Acknowledgments

I am grateful to so many people in my life who have played roles both in the writing of this book, in the creation and growth of my business, and in the living of this life that I document here. Thank you to all of you—my family, friends, clients, and colleagues.

I must start my thank yous to the person who was with me every step of the way in writing this book. Heather Doyle Fraser, you are a brilliant and compassionate genius. I've told you again and again, and I will keep telling you and everyone else that without you this book wouldn't even be a fraction of what it ended up being. You saw things in me that I couldn't see yet, and you believed in me and this book with so much trust and compassion that it made it possible to get through the times when my belief was shaky. I still can't believe you managed to get me to write poetry and publish it. I am forever changed because of our work together, and I'll never be able to thank you enough for what you have added to my life over these last few years.

To Eric, someone recently told me the only unconditional love she ever felt was from her mom and kids, because her husband could choose to leave her. I immediately thought of you and how I felt differently and how I trust in your unconditional love the most of everyone in my life. I am so lucky to have you by my side through this story and beyond. I love you, krej. 🐢

To Lily and Zoey, I love you exactly as you are, and I don't know if it's possible to even tell you how much you have taught me. Y'all are such cool people, and I love being around you. You make me a better person, and I am so lucky to be your mom. #BrittanyOboe #WhatIsNaCl 🐶🐱🤪

To my velcro dog, Bruno, for joining me on my lap so often during Writing Practice and to my dog, Vader, who played no part in this book but who is a really good boy.

To my mom and dad, I know the idea of your kid writing a memoir is terrifying, and I know this process was messy, but please know I love you so much. Thank you so much for always giving me the opportunities I wanted and for your loving presence throughout my life and my kids' lives. Thank you for putting up with my big emotions, tissue ghosts, intense competitive spirit, and messy room and garage.

To my 𝖜𝖎𝖙𝖈𝖍𝖊𝖘? Madalyn Gregory, Paige Culpepper, and Amber Hager, I couldn't have done anything I have done in the last ten years without you. You have taught me so much, especially that I am worthy of love and friendship. You've also taught me that even though I am "ruthless," "opinionated," and "messy" (your words), you'll love me anyway. See the *Three Graces* chapter for more about how much I lurve y'all.

To my *Art Connection Circle* members, thank you for believing me when I said I had something special in this program. Thanks for your trust and your vulnerability. Thank you for showing me what is possible.

To all the art teachers in the Art Class Curator community. Thank you for the brave and impactful work you do in the world. Thank you for your support of me and my business. Thank you for sharing my mission of bringing art into the hearts of the people of the world.

To all the members, past and present, of the Writing Practice led by Heather Doyle Fraser. This has become a truly sacred space for me, adding so much to my life over the last year and a half. I look forward to seeing your beautiful faces every day and sharing in this writing journey.

To Allison Crow, you have been such an important and special part of my life over the last few years. Thank you for our conversation by the pool and all the others that followed. I often feel so misunderstood by business coaches, and you always get me. You see what I am trying to do, and you helped me slog through this bug soup with such understanding and gentleness. Seeing you nearly every day in writing practice also means you are intimately entwined with this book in my memory, and I love that for us.

To Yola Mehmeti, you are pure magic, and my work with you was magic. Thanks for helping me figure out my own magic. Magic magic magic. I have the fondest memories of our hours of Voxers with me driving around missing turns and you walking through NYC in the cold in your ballet flats. I think of you every time I hear a horn honk in the distance.

To Lisa Carpenter, it's still amazing when I think about who I was when we started working together and when we finished our work together. So much has changed, and I am eternally grateful for you. I dedicate *The Opening* chapter to you.

To Carol LeBlanc, I love you to pieces in all the contexts we have been in each other's lives over the last five years. You help me through the highest highs and lowest lows of my business. Thank you for all you taught me and for being that compassionate and steady rock that I needed through all of my business growth.

To Sarah Crane, I knew I hit the therapist jackpot after our first session when you invited me to bring artworks to discuss as a way to process if I ever wanted. Writing a book is a fucking trip, and you were instrumental in helping me navigate the emotions that came up as I reprocessed my entire life in order to get these words onto the paper. Thank you so much.

To Jennifer Easterling, Rachel Lapp Whitt, Amy Davis, and Madalyn Gregory, my team. You could read this book and think there was a time where I wasn't happy working with you. That has never been true. You were the highlight. You kept my job fun, and your passion for this work and your support of our/my mission were buoys when I was so tired of swimming. Jennifer, there's not a week that goes by that I don't think about you and miss your presence in my life. Rachel, you were my first hire and have always been my biggest supporter. Thank you for being with me as I fumbled through this thing. I am so honored to have you with me again, designing this book. It's full circle for me in a way that feels so good. Thank you for not giving up on me. Amy, I know your job looks different now from when you started, but I cannot thank you enough for sticking with me through this. You are such a beautiful, grounding presence in my life. Madalyn, all the love, all the words, all the thanks, all the museum visits, all the Voxers, all the tears, all the tarot cards, all the things, forever and ever and ever.

To all of the artists who allowed me to include their work in this book, I know it's a scary idea to put your art next to the intimate details of someone's life, overlaying their story onto yours, but that's what makes art so beautiful. Thank you for being an artist. Thank you for giving of yourself so that I could grow.

To the authors of all the books I read while I wrote my book. You were part of the writing of this book in a way that is very special to me. Most of the quotes from this book came from books that I read while writing this book, and many of the books influenced this book in small and big ways. I use books just as much as art to process my life. I believe there is a hidden magic that gives you the right book at the right time, and that happened over and over in the last year and a half of writing this book. The *Jaws* chapter wouldn't exist without the beautiful and delightful *Remarkably Bright Creatures* by Shelby van Pelt. The "this is me" poem in the last chapter wouldn't exist in that form without *Girl, Woman, Other* by Bernardine Eva-risto. The part openers and cento poem wouldn't exist without *You Could Make This Place Beautiful* by Maggie Smith. That book. There are no words to convey how special that book is to me. *Tomorrow, and Tomorrow, and Tomorrow* by Gabrielle Zevin gave me so much fortitude and wisdom on the topic of creativity and failure as I worked to unpack the last few years. NK Jemisin made me realize for the first time since high school that prose poetry was a thing. I read five of her books over the course of writing this one. I saw myself and my love of art in Dave Grohl's love of music in his memoir. Tricia Hersey, in *Rest is Resistance*, gave me a permission slip to spend the last months of my life just on this book and my family. Anne Lamott made me feel less alone in the process of writing this book in *Bird by Bird*. When in periods of anxiety and difficult emotions during this process, I, of course, have my fallbacks of *Eat Pray Love* and *Big Magic* by Elizabeth Gilbert to listen to on audible over and over again. Thank you for your whole body of work, but thank you for being the soothing voice in my ear and comfort when I need to find my center or when I can't fall asleep. Thank you for all the work you do on yourself to be able to put your work out in the world. I've always been a reader, but writing a book has made me both a better reader and more in awe of anyone who has written a book. Thank you to all the authors of all the books I've loved, not just in the last few years but forever.

Thank you to you, for reading this book and for allowing me to be a part of your life during this time.

About the Author and Artist

Cindy Ingram is a writer, artist, poet, educator, and entrepreneur. Connecting with works of art and crafting innovative learning activities are her superpowers, and she has dedicated her life to bringing the magic of art connection to others.

A former art museum educator and art teacher with a B.A. in Art History from the University of Texas at Austin and an M.A. in Art Education from the University of North Texas, Cindy has supported teachers and their students through her work as founder and CEO of Art Class Curator (artclasscurator.com) since 2014. Cindy is passionate about taking art out of dark, stuffy lecture halls and out of the pretentious gatekeeping of "fine art" and into the hearts, minds, and lives of everyone. She measures her success with the volume of tears shed.

Cindy lives in Wylie, Texas with her fully-neurodiverse family, which includes her husband, two daughters, and two dogs (the dogs are self-diagnosed). She delights in all things science, philosophy, art, and psychology and unironically marveling about thoughts, ideas, and feelings. When she is not on the couch playing video games with a dog on her lap, you'll find her reading, traveling, playing board games with friends, watching musical theater, creating mixed media collages in her art journal, and, of course, visiting art museums.

If you would like to experience more of Cindy's talents and skill, check out her podcast *Art and Self with Cindy Ingram* (artandself.com/podcast), or Cindy's programs *Curated Connections* (for art teachers—artclasscurator.com/join) and *The Art Connection Circle* (artandself.com/circle). In her work with groups and individual clients, Cindy combines her art and teaching expertise with her obsession of philosophy, personal development, and coaching to create a unique take on both how to engage with art and how to use art as a tool for self discovery, clarity, and action.

Made in the USA
Coppell, TX
27 November 2023

24823762R10125